HOLT McDOUGAL

Introduction to Geography

Christopher L. Salter

HISTORY™

HOLT McDOUGAL

HOUGHTON MIFFLIN HARCOURT

Author

Dr. Christopher L. Salter

Dr. Christopher L. "Kit" Salter is Professor Emeritus of geography and former Chair of the Department of Geography at the University of Missouri. He did his undergraduate work at Oberlin College and received both his M.A. and Ph.D. degrees in geography from the University of California at Berkeley.

Dr. Salter is one of the country's leading figures in geography education. In the 1980s he helped found the national Geographic Alliance network to promote geography education in all 50 states. In the 1990s Dr. Salter was Co-Chair of the National Geography Standards Project, a group of distinguished geographers who created *Geography for Life* in 1994, the document outlining national standards in geography. In 1990 Dr. Salter received the National Geographic Society's first-ever Distinguished Geography Educator Award. In 1992 he received the George Miller Award for distinguished service in geography education from the National Council for Geographic Education. In 2006 Dr. Salter was awarded Lifetime Achievement Honors by the Association of American Geographers for his transformation of geography education.

Over the years, Dr. Salter has written or edited more than 150 articles and books on cultural geography, China, field work, and geography education. His primary interests lie in the study of the human and physical forces that create the cultural landscape, both nationally and globally.

ISBN-13 978-0-547-48490-7

4 5 6 7 8 9 10 0918 19 18 17 16 15 14 13

4500419085   B C D E F G

Reviewers

Academic Reviewers

Elizabeth Chako, Ph.D.
Department of Geography
The George Washington
  University

Altha J. Cravey, Ph.D.
Department of Geography
University of North Carolina

Eugene Cruz-Uribe, Ph.D.
Department of History
Northern Arizona University

Toyin Falola, Ph.D.
Department of History
University of Texas

Sandy Freitag, Ph.D.
Director, Monterey Bay History
  and Cultures Project
Division of Social Sciences
University of California,
  Santa Cruz

Oliver Froehling, Ph.D.
Department of Geography
University of Kentucky

Reuel Hanks, Ph.D.
Department of Geography
Oklahoma State University

Phil Klein, Ph.D.
Department of Geography
University of Northern Colorado

B. Ikubolajeh Logan, Ph.D.
Department of Geography
Pennsylvania State University

Marc Van De Mieroop, Ph.D.
Department of History
Columbia University
New York, New York

Christopher Merrett, Ph.D.
Department of History
Western Illinois University

Jesse P. H. Poon, Ph.D.
Department of Geography
University at Buffalo–SUNY

Thomas R. Paradise, Ph.D.
Department of Geosciences
University of Arkansas

Robert Schoch, Ph.D.
CGS Division of Natural Science
Boston University

Derek Shanahan, Ph.D.
Department of Geography
Millersville University
Millersville, Pennsylvania

David Shoenbrun, Ph.D.
Department of History
Northwestern University
Evanston, Illinois

Sean Terry, Ph.D.
Department of Interdisciplinary
  Studies, Geography and
  Environmental Studies
Drury University
Springfield, Missouri

Educational Reviewers

Carla Freel
Hoover Middle School
Merced, California

Dennis Neel Durbin
Dyersburg High School
Dyersburg, Tennessee

Tina Nelson
Deer Park Middle School
Randallstown, Maryland

Don Polston
Lebanon Middle School
Lebanon, Indiana

Robert Valdez
Pioneer Middle School
Tustin, California

Teacher Review Panel

Heather Green
LaVergne Middle School
LaVergne, Tennessee

John Griffin
Wilbur Middle School
Wichita, Kansas

Rosemary Hall
Derby Middle School
Birmingham, Michigan

Rose King
Yeatman-Liddell School
St. Louis, Missouri

Mary Liebl
Wichita Public Schools USD 259
Wichita, Kansas

Jennifer Smith
Lake Wood Middle School
Overland Park, Kansas

Melinda Stephani
Wake County Schools
Raleigh, North Carolina

Introduction to Geography

Introduction to Geography 1

References

Reading Social Studies

Atlas

Available @

⤴ hmhsocialstudies.com

- Facts About the World
- Regions of the World Handbook
- Standardized Test-Taking Strategies
- Economics Handbook

HISTORY
MADE EVERY DAY.

HISTORY™ is the leading destination for revealing, award-winning, original non-fiction series and event-driven specials that connect history with viewers in an informative, immersive and entertaining manner across multiple platforms. HISTORY is part of A&E Television Networks (AETN), a joint venture of Hearst Corporation, Disney/ABC Television Group and NBC Universal, an award-winning, international media company that also includes, among others, A&E Network™, BIO™, and History International™.

HISTORY programming greatly appeals to educators and young people who are drawn into the visual stories our documentaries tell. Our Education Department has a long-standing record in providing teachers and students with curriculum resources that bring the past to life in the classroom. Our content covers a diverse variety of subjects, including American and world history, government, economics, the natural and applied sciences, arts, literature and the humanities, health and guidance, and even pop culture.

The HISTORY website, located at **www.history.com**, is the definitive historical online source that delivers entertaining and informative content featuring broadband video, interactive timelines, maps, games, podcasts and more.

"We strive to engage, inspire and encourage the love of learning..."

Since its founding in 1995, HISTORY has demonstrated a commitment to providing the highest quality resources for educators. We develop multimedia resources for K–12 schools, two- and four-year colleges, government agencies, and other organizations by drawing on the award-winning documentary programming of A&E Television Networks. We strive to engage, inspire and encourage the love of learning by connecting with students in an informative and compelling manner. To help achieve this goal, we have formed a partnership with Houghton Mifflin Harcourt.

The Idea Book for Educators

Classroom resources that bring the past to life

Live webcasts

HISTORY Take a Veteran to School Day

In addition to premium video-based resources, **HISTORY** has extensive offerings for teachers, parents, and students to use in the classroom and in their in-home educational activities, including:

▶ *The Idea Book for Educators* is a biannual teacher's magazine, featuring guides and info on the latest happenings in history education to help keep teachers on the cutting edge.

▶ **HISTORY Classroom (www.history.com/classroom)** is an interactive website that serves as a portal for history educators nationwide. Streaming videos on topics ranging from the Roman aqueducts to the civil rights movement connect with classroom curricula.

▶ **HISTORY email newsletters** feature updates and supplements to our award-winning programming relevant to the classroom with links to teaching guides and video clips on a variety of topics, special offers, and more.

▶ **Live webcasts** are featured each year as schools tune in via streaming video.

▶ **HISTORY Take a Veteran to School Day** connects veterans with young people in our schools and communities nationwide.

In addition to **HOUGHTON MIFFLIN HARCOURT**, our partners include the *Library of Congress*, the *Smithsonian Institution*, *National History Day*, *The Gilder Lehrman Institute of American History*, the *Organization of American Historians*, and many more. HISTORY video is also featured in museums throughout America and in over 70 other historic sites worldwide.

Geography and Map Skills Handbook

Contents

Throughout this textbook, you will be studying the world's people, places, and landscapes. One of the main tools you will use is the map—the primary tool of geographers. To help you begin your studies, this Geography and Map Skills Handbook explains some of the basic features of maps. For example, it explains how maps are made, how to read them, and how they can show the round surface of Earth on a flat piece of paper. This handbook will also introduce you to some of the types of maps you will study later in this book. In addition, you will learn about the different kinds of features on Earth and about how geographers use themes and elements to study the world.

↗ hmhsocialstudies.com **INTERACTIVE MAPS**

Geography Skills With map zone geography skills, you can go online to find interactive versions of the key maps in this book. Explore these interactive maps to learn and practice important map skills and bring geography to life.

You can access all of the interactive maps in this book through the Interactive Student Edition at

↗ hmhsocialstudies.com

Mapping the Earth
Using Latitude and Longitude

A **globe** is a scale model of the Earth. It is useful for showing the entire Earth or studying large areas of Earth's surface.

To study the world, geographers use a pattern of imaginary lines that circles the globe in east-west and north-south directions. It is called a **grid**. The intersection of these imaginary lines helps us find places on Earth.

The east-west lines in the grid are lines of **latitude**, which you can see on the diagram. Lines of latitude are called **parallels** because they are always parallel to each other. These imaginary lines measure distance north and south of the **equator**. The equator is an imaginary line that circles the globe halfway between the North and South Poles. Parallels measure distance from the equator in **degrees**. The symbol for degrees is °. Degrees are further divided into **minutes**. The symbol for minutes is ´. There are 60 minutes in a degree. Parallels north of the equator are labeled with an N. Those south of the equator are labeled with an S.

The north-south imaginary lines are lines of **longitude**. Lines of longitude are called **meridians**. These imaginary lines pass through the poles. They measure distance east and west of the **prime meridian**. The prime meridian is an imaginary line that runs through Greenwich, England. It represents 0° longitude.

Lines of latitude range from 0°, for locations on the equator, to 90°N or 90°S, for locations at the poles. Lines of longitude range from 0° on the prime meridian to 180° on a meridian in the mid-Pacific Ocean. Meridians west of the prime meridian to 180° are labeled with a W. Those east of the prime meridian to 180° are labeled with an E. Using latitude and longitude, geographers can identify the exact location of any place on Earth.

Lines of Latitude

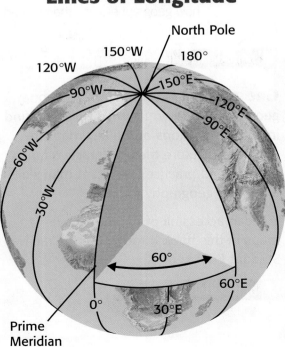

Lines of Longitude

The equator divides the globe into two halves, called **hemispheres**. The half north of the equator is the Northern Hemisphere. The southern half is the Southern Hemisphere. The prime meridian and the 180° meridian divide the world into the Eastern Hemisphere and the Western Hemisphere. Look at the diagrams on this page. They show each of these four hemispheres.

Earth's land surface is divided into seven large landmasses, called **continents**. These continents are also shown on the diagrams on this page. Landmasses smaller than continents and completely surrounded by water are called **islands**.

Geographers organize Earth's water surface into major regions too. The largest is the world ocean. Geographers divide the world ocean into the Pacific Ocean, the Atlantic Ocean, the Indian Ocean, the Arctic Ocean, and the Southern Ocean. Lakes and seas are smaller bodies of water.

Northern Hemisphere

Southern Hemisphere

Western Hemisphere

Eastern Hemisphere

Mapmaking
Understanding Map Projections

A **map** is a flat diagram of all or part of Earth's surface. Mapmakers have created different ways of showing our round planet on flat maps. These different ways are called **map projections**. Because Earth is round, there is no way to show it accurately on a flat map. All flat maps are distorted in some way. Mapmakers must choose the type of map projection that is best for their purposes. Many map projections are one of three kinds: cylindrical, conic, or flat-plane.

Paper cylinder

Mercator projection

Cylindrical Projections

Cylindrical projections are based on a cylinder wrapped around the globe. The cylinder touches the globe only at the equator. The meridians are pulled apart and are parallel to each other instead of meeting at the poles. This causes landmasses near the poles to appear larger than they really are. The map below is a Mercator projection, one type of cylindrical projection. The Mercator projection is useful for navigators because it shows true direction and shape. However, it distorts the size of land areas near the poles.

Conic Projections

Conic projections are based on a cone placed over the globe. A conic projection is most accurate along the lines of latitude where it touches the globe. It retains almost true shape and size. Conic projections are most useful for showing areas that have long east-west dimensions, such as the United States.

Paper cone

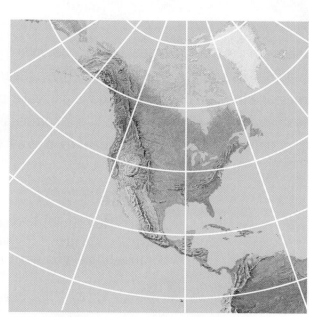

Conic projection

Flat-plane Projections

Flat-plane projections are based on a plane touching the globe at one point, such as at the North Pole or South Pole. A flat-plane projection is useful for showing true direction for airplane pilots and ship navigators. It also shows true area. However, it distorts the true shapes of landmasses.

Flat-plane projection

Flat plane

Map Essentials
How to Read a Map

Maps are like messages sent out in code. To help us translate the code, mapmakers provide certain features. These features help us understand the message they are presenting about a particular part of the world. Of these features, almost all maps have a title, a compass rose, a scale, and a legend. The map below has these four features, plus a fifth—a locator map.

1 Title

A map's **title** shows what the subject of the map is. The map title is usually the first thing you should look at when studying a map, because it tells you what the map is trying to show.

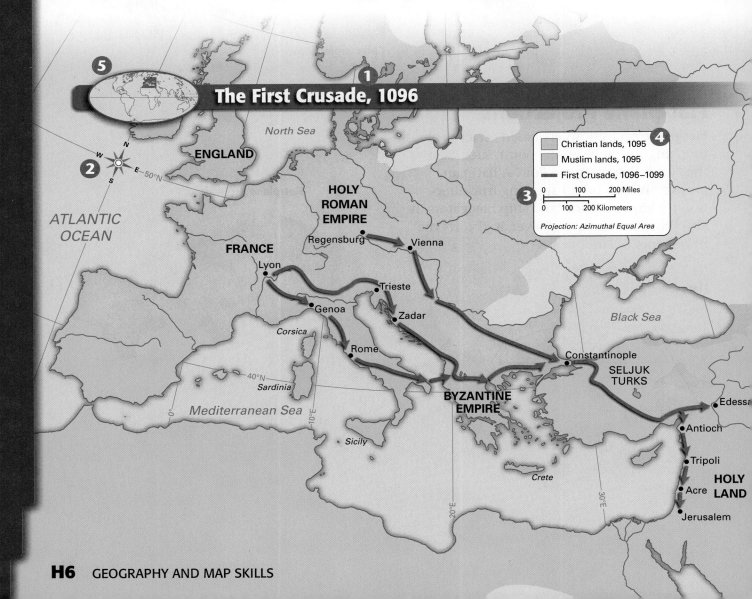

The First Crusade, 1096

Christian lands, 1095
Muslim lands, 1095
First Crusade, 1096–1099

0   100   200 Miles
0   100   200 Kilometers

Projection: Azimuthal Equal Area

North Sea
ENGLAND
ATLANTIC OCEAN
50°N
HOLY ROMAN EMPIRE
FRANCE
Lyon
Regensburg
Vienna
Trieste
Genoa
Zadar
Corsica
Rome
Black Sea
Constantinople
SELJUK TURKS
40°N
Sardinia
BYZANTINE EMPIRE
Mediterranean Sea
Sicily
Edessa
Antioch
Crete
Tripoli
HOLY LAND
Acre
Jerusalem
10°E
20°E
30°E

❷ Compass Rose

A directional indicator shows which way north, south, east, and west lie on the map. Some mapmakers use a "north arrow," which points toward the North Pole. Remember, "north" is not always at the top of a map. The way a map is drawn and the location of directions on that map depend on the perspective of the mapmaker. Most maps in this textbook indicate direction by using a compass rose. A **compass rose** has arrows that point to all four principal directions.

❸ Scale

Mapmakers use scales to represent the distances between points on a map. Scales may appear on maps in several different forms. The maps in this textbook provide a **bar scale**. Scales give distances in miles and kilometers.

To find the distance between two points on the map, place a piece of paper so that the edge connects the two points. Mark the location of each point on the paper with a line or dot. Then, compare the distance between the two dots with the map's bar scale. The number on the top of the scale gives the distance in miles. The number on the bottom gives the distance in kilometers. Because the distances are given in large intervals, you may have to approximate the actual distance on the scale.

❹ Legend

The **legend**, or key, explains what the symbols on the map represent. Point symbols are used to specify the location of things, such as cities, that do not take up much space on the map. Some legends show colors that represent certain features like empires or other regions. Other maps might have legends with symbols or colors that represent features such as roads. Legends can also show economic resources, land use, population density, and climate.

❺ Locator Map

A **locator map** shows where in the world the area on the map is located. The area shown on the main map is shown in red on the locator map. The locator map also shows surrounding areas so the map reader can see how the information on the map relates to neighboring lands.

Working with Maps
Using Different Kinds of Maps

As you study the world's regions and countries, you will use a variety of maps. Political maps and physical maps are two of the most common types of maps you will study. In addition, you will use special-purpose maps. These maps might show climate, population, resources, ancient empires, or other topics.

Political Maps

Political maps show the major political features of a region. These features include country borders, capital cities, and other places. Political maps use different colors to represent countries, and capital cities are often shown with a special star symbol.

Caribbean South America: Political

ATLANTIC OCEAN

Barranquilla
Cartagena
Maracaibo
Valencia
Caracas
TRINIDAD AND TOBAGO
10°N
Lake Maracaibo
PANAMA
Orinoco River
VENEZUELA
Georgetown
Paramaribo
Medellín
GUYANA
Cayenne
PACIFIC OCEAN
Bogotá
Orinoco River
SURINAME
FRENCH GUIANA (FRANCE)
Cali
COLOMBIA
0° Equator
Rio Negro
ECUADOR
PERU
Amazon River
Putumayo River
Magdalena River
Cauca River

- ✪ National capital
- ★ Other capitals
- ● Other cities

0   100   200 Miles
0   100   200 Kilometers
Projection: Azimuthal Equal-Area

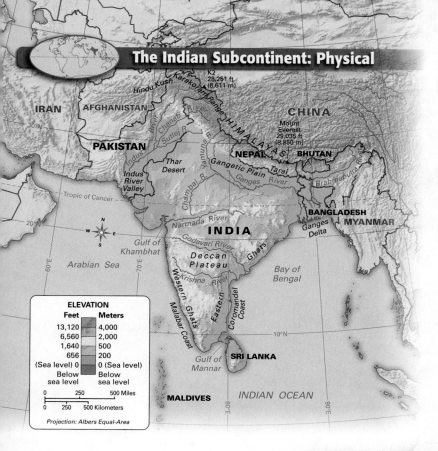

The Indian Subcontinent: Physical

IRAN
AFGHANISTAN
PAKISTAN
CHINA
Hindu Kush
Karakoram Range
K2
28,251 ft
(8,611 m)
HIMALAYAS
Mount Everest
29,035 ft
(8,850 m)
Indus River
Chenab River
Sutlej R.
NEPAL
BHUTAN
Thar Desert
Yamuna R.
Gangetic Plain
Tarai
Ganges River
Brahmaputra River
MYANMAR
BANGLADESH
Tropic of Cancer
Narmada River
Chambal R.
INDIA
Ganges Delta
Indus River Valley
30°N
20°N
Gulf of Khambhat
Godavari River
Deccan Plateau
Ghats
Bay of Bengal
60°E
70°E
Arabian Sea
Krishna River
Western Ghats
Eastern Ghats
Coromandel Coast
10°N
Malabar Coast
Gulf of Mannar
SRI LANKA
MALDIVES
INDIAN OCEAN
80°E
90°E

ELEVATION

Feet	Meters
13,120	4,000
6,560	2,000
1,640	500
656	200
(Sea level) 0	0 (Sea level)
Below sea level	Below sea level

0   250   500 Miles
0   250   500 Kilometers

Projection: Albers Equal-Area

Physical Maps

Physical maps show the major physical features of a region. These features may include mountain ranges, rivers, oceans, islands, deserts, and plains. Often, these maps use different colors to represent different elevations of land. As a result, the map reader can easily see which areas are high elevations, like mountains, and which areas are lower.

Special-Purpose Maps

Special-purpose maps focus on one special topic, such as climate, resources, or population. These maps present information on the topic that is particularly important in the region. Depending on the type of special-purpose map, the information may be shown with different colors, arrows, dots, or other symbols.

West Africa: Climate

MAURITANIA
MALI
NIGER
CHAD
SENEGAL
GAMBIA
GUINEA
BURKINA FASO
BENIN
NIGERIA
Niger River
GUINEA-BISSAU
SIERRA LEONE
CÔTE D'IVOIRE
LIBERIA
GHANA
TOGO
Gulf of Guinea
ATLANTIC OCEAN
0° Equator
20°N
10°N
10°W
0°
10°S

Climate Types

Humid tropical	Desert
Tropical savanna	Steppe

0   400   800 Miles
0   400   800 Kilometers

Projection: Azimuthal Equal-Area

Using Maps in Geography The different kinds of maps in this textbook will help you study and understand geography. By working with these maps, you will see what the physical geography of places is like, where people live, and how the world has changed over time.

Geographic Dictionary

OCEAN
a large body of water

CORAL REEF
an ocean ridge made up of
skeletal remains of tiny sea animals

GULF
a large part of
the ocean that
extends into land

PENINSULA
an area of land that sticks
out into a lake or ocean

ISTHMUS
a narrow piece of land
connecting two larger
land areas

BAY
part of a large
body of water
that is smaller
than a gulf

ISLAND
an area of land
surrounded entirely
by water

DELTA
an area where a
river deposits soil
into the ocean

STRAIT
a narrow body of
water connecting two
larger bodies of water

SINKHOLE
a circular depression
formed when the roof
of a cave collapses

WETLAND
an area of land
covered by
shallow water

RIVER
a natural flow of
water that runs
through the land

LAKE
an inland body
of water

FOREST
an area of densely
wooded land

COAST
an area of land near the ocean

MOUNTAIN
an area of rugged land that generally rises higher than 2,000 feet

VALLEY
an area of low land between hills or mountains

GLACIER
a large area of slow-moving ice

VOLCANO
an opening in Earth's crust where lava, ash, and gases erupt

CANYON
a deep, narrow valley with steep walls

HILL
a rounded, elevated area of land smaller than a mountain

PLAIN
a nearly flat area

DUNE
a hill of sand shaped by wind

OASIS
an area in the desert with a water source

DESERT
an extremely dry area with little water and few plants

PLATEAU
a large, flat, elevated area of land

Themes and Essential Elements of Geography

by Dr. Christopher L. Salter

To study the world, geographers have identified 5 key themes, 6 essential elements, and 18 geography standards.

"How should we teach and learn about geography?" Professional geographers have worked hard over the years to answer this important question.

In 1984 a group of geographers identified the 5 Themes of Geography. These themes did a wonderful job of laying the groundwork for good classroom geography. Teachers used the 5 Themes in class, and geographers taught workshops on how to apply them in the world.

By the early 1990s, however, some geographers felt the 5 Themes were too broad. They created the 18 Geography Standards and the 6 Essential Elements. The 18 Geography Standards include more detailed information about what geography is, and the 6 Essential Elements are like a bridge between the 5 Themes and 18 Standards.

Look at the chart to the right. It shows how each of the 5 Themes connects to the Essential Elements and Standards. For example, the theme of Location is related to The World in Spatial Terms and the first three Standards. Study the chart carefully to see how the other themes, elements, and Standards are related.

The last Essential Element and the last two Standards cover The Uses of Geography. These key parts of geography were not covered by the 5 Themes. They will help you see how geography has influenced the past, present, and future.

5 Themes of Geography

Location The theme of location describes where something is.

Place Place describes the features that make a site unique.

Regions Regions are areas that share common characteristics.

Movement This theme looks at how and why people and things move.

Human-Environment Interaction People interact with their environment in many ways.

Essential Elements

 Geography Standards

1. How to use maps and other tools
2. How to use mental maps to organize information
3. How to analyze the spatial organization of people, places, and environments

I. **The World in Spatial Terms**

4. The physical and human characteristics of places
5. How people create regions to interpret Earth
6. How culture and experience influence people's perceptions of places and regions

II. **Places and Regions**

7. The physical processes that shape Earth's surface
8. The distribution of ecosystems on Earth

9. The characteristics, distribution, and migration of human populations
10. The complexity of Earth's cultural mosaics
11. The patterns and networks of economic interdependence on Earth
12. The patterns of human settlement
13. The forces of cooperation and conflict

III. **Physical Systems**

IV. **Human Systems**

14. How human actions modify the physical environment
15. How physical systems affect human systems
16. The distribution and meaning of resources

V. **Environment and Society**

17. How to apply geography to interpret the past
18. How to apply geography to interpret the present and plan for the future

VI. **The Uses of Geography**

Become an Active Reader

Did you ever think you would begin reading your social studies book by reading about *reading*? Actually, it makes better sense than you might think. You would probably make sure you knew some soccer skills and strategies before playing in a game. Similarly, you need to know something about reading skills and strategies before reading your social studies book. In other words, you need to make sure you know what-ever you need to know in order to read this book successfully.

Tip #1

Read Everything on the Page!

You can't follow the directions on the cake-mix box if you don't know where the directions are! Cake-mix boxes always have directions on them telling you how many eggs to add or how long to bake the cake. But, if you can't find that information, it doesn't matter that it is there.

Likewise, this book is filled with information that will help you understand what you are reading. If you don't study that information, however, it might as well not be there. Let's take a look at some of the places where you'll find important information in this book.

The Chapter Opener
The chapter opener gives you a brief overview of what you will learn in the chapter. You can use this information to prepare to read the chapter.

The Section Openers
Before you begin to read each section, preview the information under What You Will Learn. There you'll find the main ideas of the section and key terms that are important in it. Knowing what you are looking for before you start reading can improve your understanding.

Boldfaced Words
Those words are important and are defined somewhere on the page where they appear—either right there in the sentence or over in the side margin.

Maps, Charts, and Artwork
These things are not there just to take up space or look good! Study them and read the information beside them. It will help you understand the information in the chapter.

Questions at the End of Sections
At the end of each section, you will find questions that will help you decide whether you need to go back and re-read any parts before moving on. If you can't answer a question, that is your cue to go back and re-read.

Questions at the End of the Chapter
Answer the questions at the end of each chapter, even if your teacher doesn't ask you to. These questions are there to help you figure out what you need to review.

Tip #2

Use the Reading Skills and Strategies in Your Textbook

Good readers use a number of skills and strategies to make sure they understand what they are reading. In this textbook you will find help with important reading skills and strategies such as "Using Prior Knowledge" and "Understanding Main Ideas."

We teach the reading skills and strategies in several ways. Use these activities and lessons and you will become a better reader.

- First, on the opening page of every chapter we identify and explain the reading skill or strategy you will focus on as you work through the chapter. In fact, these activities are called "Focus on Reading."

- Second, as you can see in the example at right, we tell you where to go for more help. The back of the book has a reading handbook with a full-page practice lesson to match the reading skill or strategy in every chapter.

- Third, we give you short practice activities and examples as you read the chapter. These activities and examples show up in the margin of your book. Again, look for the words, "Focus on Reading."

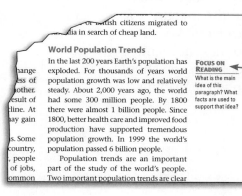

World Population Trends

In the last 200 years Earth's population has exploded. For thousands of years world population growth was low and relatively steady. About 2,000 years ago, the world had some 300 million people. By 1800 there were almost 1 billion people. Since 1800, better health care and improved food production have supported tremendous population growth. In 1999 the world's population passed 6 billion people.

Population trends are an important part of the study of the world's people. Two important population trends are clear

FOCUS ON READING
What is the main idea of this paragraph? What facts are used to support that idea?

- Finally, we provide another practice activity in the Chapter Review at the end of every chapter. That activity gives you one more chance to make sure you know how to use the reading skill or strategy.

FOCUS ON READING AND WRITING

19. **Using Prior Knowledge** Create a chart with three columns. In the first column, list what you knew about geography before you read the chapter. In the second column, list what you learned in the chapter. In the third column, list questions that you now have about geography.

20. **Writing Your Job Description** Review your notes on the different jobs geographers do. Then write your job description. You should begin your description by explaining why the job is important. Then identify the job's tasks and responsibilities. Finally, tell what kind of person might do well as a geographer.

Tip #3

Pay Attention to Vocabulary

It is no fun to read something when you don't know what the words mean, but you can't learn new words if you only use or read the words you already know. In this book, we know we have probably used some words you don't know. But, we have followed a pattern as we have used more difficult words.

- First, at the beginning of each section you will find a list of key terms that you will need to know. Be on the lookout for those words as you read through the section. You will find that we have defined those words right there in the paragraph where they are used. Look for a word that is in boldface with its definition highlighted in yellow.

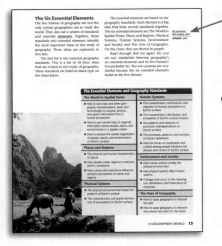

- Second, when we use a word that is important in all classes, not just social studies, we define it in the margin under the heading Academic Vocabulary. You will run into these academic words in other textbooks, so you should learn what they mean while reading this book.

Tip #4

Read Like a Skilled Reader

You won't be able to climb to the top of Mount Everest if you do not train! If you want to make it to the top of Mount Everest then you must start training to climb that huge mountain.

Training is also necessary to become a good reader. You will never get better at reading your social studies book—or any book for that matter—unless you spend some time thinking about how to be a better reader.

Skilled readers do the following:

1. They preview what they are supposed to read before they actually begin reading. When previewing, they look for vocabulary words, titles of sections, information in the margin, or maps or charts they should study.

2. They get ready to take some notes while reading by dividing their notebook paper into two parts. They title one side "Notes from the Chapter" and the other side "Questions or Comments I Have."

3. As they read, they complete their notes.

4. They read like **active readers**. The Active Reading list below shows you what that means.

5. Finally, they use clues in the text to help them figure out where the text is going. The best clues are called signal words. These are words that help you identify chronological order, causes and effects, or comparisons and contrasts.

Chronological Order Signal Words: *first, second, third, before, after, later, next, following that, earlier, subsequently, finally*

Cause and Effect Signal Words: *because of, due to, as a result of, the reason for, therefore, consequently, so, basis for*

Comparison/Contrast Signal Words: *likewise, also, as well as, similarly, on the other hand*

Active Reading

There are three ways to read a book: You can be a turn-the-pages-no-matter-what type of reader. These readers just keep on turning pages whether or not they understand what they are reading. Or, you can be a stop-watch-and-listen kind of reader. These readers know that if they wait long enough, someone will tell them what they need to know. Or, you can be an active reader. These readers know that it is up to them to figure out what the text means. Active readers do the following as they read:

Predict what will happen next based on what has already happened. When your predictions don't match what happens in the text, re-read the confusing parts.

Question what is happening as you read. Constantly ask yourself why things have happened, what things mean, and what caused certain events. Jot down notes about the questions you can't answer.

Summarize what you are reading frequently. Do not try to summarize the entire chapter! Read a bit and then summarize it. Then read on.

Connect what is happening in the section you're reading to what you have already read.

Clarify your understanding. Be sure that you understand what you are reading by stopping occasionally to ask yourself whether you are confused by anything. Sometimes you might need to re-read to clarify. Other times you might need to read further and collect more information before you can understand. Still other times you might need to ask the teacher to help you with what is confusing you.

Visualize what is happening in the text. In other words, try to see the events or places in your mind. It might help you to draw maps, make charts, or jot down notes about what you are reading as you try to visualize the action in the text.

Social Studies Words

As you read this textbook, you will be more successful if you learn the meanings of the words on this page. You will come across these words many times in your social studies classes, like geography and history. Read through these words now to become familiar with them before you begin your studies.

Social Studies Words

WORDS ABOUT TIME

AD	refers to dates after the birth of Jesus
BC	refers to dates before Jesus's birth
BCE	refers to dates before Jesus's birth, stands for "before the common era"
CE	refers to dates after Jesus's birth, stands for "common era"
century	a period of 100 years
decade	a period of 10 years
era	a period of time
millennium	a period of 1,000 years

WORDS ABOUT THE WORLD

climate	the weather conditions in a certain area over a long period of time
geography	the study of the world's people, places, and landscapes
physical features	features on Earth's surface, such as mountains and rivers
region	an area with one or more features that make it different from surrounding areas
resources	materials found on Earth that people need and value

WORDS ABOUT PEOPLE

anthropology	the study of people and cultures
archaeology	the study of the past based on what people left behind
citizen	a person who lives under the control of a government
civilization	the way of life of people in a particular place or time
culture	the knowledge, beliefs, customs, and values of a group of people
custom	a repeated practice or tradition
economics	the study of the production and use of goods and services
economy	any system in which people make and exchange goods and services
government	the body of officials and groups that run an area
history	the study of the past
politics	the process of running a government
religion	a system of beliefs in one or more gods or spirits
society	a group of people who share common traditions
trade	the exchange of goods or services

Academic Words

What are academic words? They are important words used in all of your classes, not just social studies. You will see these words in other textbooks, so you should learn what they mean while reading this book. Review this list now. You will use these words again in the chapters of this book.

Academic Words

consequences	the effects of a particular event or events	**innovation**	a new idea or way of doing something
distinct	clearly different and separate	**structure**	the way something is set up or organized
element	the part of a particular event or events	**traditional**	customary, time-honored
factor	cause		

Academic Words features provide definitions for important terms that will help you understand social studies content.

The highest level of economic activity, quaternary industry, involves the research and distribution of information. People making a living at this level work with information rather than goods, and often have specialized knowledge and skills. Architects, lawyers, and scientists all work in quaternary industries.

Economic Systems

Just as economic activities are organized into different types, so are our economic systems. Economic systems can be divided into three types: traditional, market, and command. Most countries today use a mix of these economic systems.

One economic system is a **traditional** economy, a system in which people grow their own food and make their own goods. Trade may take place through barter, or the exchange of goods without the use of money. Rural and remote communities often have a mostly traditional economy.

ACADEMIC VOCABULARY
traditional
customary, time-honored

The most common economic system used around the world today is a market economy. A **market economy** is a system based on private ownership, free trade, and competition. Individuals and businesses are free to buy and sell what they wish. Prices are determined by the supply and demand for goods. This is sometimes called capitalism. The United States is one of many countries that use this system.

A third system is a **command economy**, a system in which the central government makes all economic decisions. The government decides what goods to produce, how much to produce, and what prices will be. While no country has a purely command economy, the economies of North Korea and Cuba are close to it. The Communist governments of these nations own and control most businesses.

READING CHECK Summarizing What economic systems are used in the world today?

THE WORLD ALMANAC Facts about Countries A Developed and a Developing Country

Australia	
Per Capita GDP (U.S. $):	$38,100
Life Expectancy at Birth:	81.6
Literacy Rate:	93.4%
Physicians Per 10,000 People:	25

Afghanistan	
Per Capita GDP (U.S. $):	$700
Life Expectancy at Birth:	44.2
Literacy Rate:	28%
Physicians Per 10,000 People:	2

Contrasting How does the quality of life in Afghanistan differ from that in Australia?

hmhsocialstudies.com

Economic Development

Economic systems and activities affect a country's economic development, or the level of economic growth and quality of life. Geographers often group countries into two basic categories—developed and developing countries—based on their level of economic development.

Economic Indicators

Geographers use economic indicators, or measures of a country's wealth, to decide if a country is developed or developing. One such measure is gross domestic product. **Gross domestic product (GDP)** is the value of all goods and services produced within a country in a single year. Another indicator is a country's per capita GDP, or the total GDP divided by the number of people in a country. As you can see in the chart, per capita GDP allows us to compare incomes among countries. Other indicators include the level of industrialization and overall quality of life. In other words, we look at the types of industries and technology a country has, in addition to its level of health care and education.

Developed and Developing Countries

Many of the world's wealthiest and most powerful nations are **developed countries**, countries with strong economies and a high quality of life. Developed countries like Germany and the United States have a high per capita GDP and high levels of industrialization. Their health care and education systems are among the best in the world. Many people in developed countries have access to technology.

The world's poorer nations are known as **developing countries**, countries with less productive economies and a lower quality of life. Almost two-thirds of the people in the world live in developing countries. These developing countries have a lower per capita GDP than developed countries. Most of their citizens work in farming or other primary industries. Although these countries typically have large cities, much of their population still lives in rural areas. People in developing countries usually have less access to health care or technology. Guatemala, Nigeria, and Afghanistan are all developing countries.

READING CHECK Analyzing What factors separate developed and developing countries?

SUMMARY AND PREVIEW The world's countries have different governments, economies, and levels of development. Next, you will learn how people are linked in a global community.

Section 3 Assessment hmhsocialstudies.com online quiz

Reviewing Ideas, Terms, and Places
1. a. Identify What are some different types of government?
   b. Elaborate Under which type of government would you most want to live? Why?
2. a. Describe What are the levels of economic activity?
   b. Evaluate Which economic system do you think is best? Explain your answer.
3. a. Define What is **gross domestic product**?
   b. Contrast In what ways do **developed countries** differ from **developing countries**?

Critical Thinking
4. Categorizing Draw a chart like the one here. Use the chart and your notes to identify the different governments, economies, and levels of economic development in the world today.

Types of Government	Economic Systems	Economic Development

FOCUS ON WRITING
5. Thinking about Government and Economy What kinds of images and words could you use to present the main ideas behind the world's governments and economies?

Making This Book Work for You

Studying geography will be easy for you with this textbook. Take a few minutes now to become familiar with the easy-to-use structure and special features of your book. See how it will make geography come alive for you!

Your book begins with a satellite image of the world. You can explore this image to begin your study of geography.

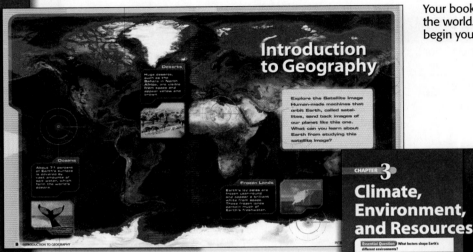

Chapter

Each chapter includes an introduction, a Social Studies Skills activity, Chapter Review pages, and a Standardized Test Practice page.

Reading Social Studies Chapter reading lessons give you skills and practice to help you read the textbook. More help with each lesson can be found in the back of the book. Margin notes and questions in the chapter make sure you understand the reading skill.

Social Studies Skills The Social Studies Skills lessons give you an opportunity to learn, practice, and apply an important skill. Chapter Review questions then follow up on what you learned.

Section

The section opener pages include Main Ideas, an overarching Big Idea, and Key Terms and Places. In addition, each section includes these special features.

If YOU Lived There . . . Each section begins with a situation for you to respond to, placing you in a place that relates to the content you will be studying in the section.

Building Background Building Background connects what will be covered in each section with what you already know.

Short Sections of Content The information in each section is organized into small chunks of text that you can easily understand.

Taking Notes Suggested graphic organizers help you read and take notes on the important ideas in the section.

SECTION 1

Studying Geography

What You Will Learn...

Main Ideas
1. Geography is the study of the world, its people, and the landscapes they create.
2. Geographers look at the world in many different ways.
3. Maps and other tools help geographers study the planet.

The Big Idea
The study of geography and the use of geographic tools helps us view the world in new ways.

Key Terms
geography, p. 4
landscape, p. 4
social science, p. 5
region, p. 6
map, p. 8
globe, p. 8

hmhsocialstudies.com
TAKING NOTES
Use the graphic organizer online to record details about geography and what geographers do.

If YOU lived there...
You have just moved to Miami, Florida, from your old home in Pennsylvania. Everything seems very different—from the weather and the trees to the way people dress and talk. Even the streets and buildings look different. One day you get an e-mail from a friend at your old school. "What's it like living there?" he asks.

How will you describe your new home?

BUILDING BACKGROUND Often, when you are telling someone about a place they have never been, what you are describing is the place's geography. What the place looks like, what kind of weather it has, and how people live there are all parts of its geography.

What Is Geography?
Think about the place where you live. What does the land look like? Are there tall mountains nearby, or is the land so flat that you can see for miles? Is the ground covered with bright green grass and trees, or is the area part of a sandy desert?

Now think about the weather in your area. What is it like? Does it get really hot in the summer? Do you see snow every winter? How much does it rain? Do tornadoes ever strike?

Finally, think about the people who live in your town or city. Do they live mostly in apartments or houses? Do most people own cars, or do they get around town on buses or trains? What kinds of jobs do adults in your town have? Were most of the people you know born in your town, or did they move there?

The things that you have been thinking about are part of your area's geography. **Geography** is the study of the world, its people, and the landscapes they create. To a geographer, a place's **landscape** is all the human and physical features that make it unique. When they study the world's landscapes, geographers ask questions much like the ones you just asked yourself.

4 CHAPTER 1

Meteorology is the study of weather. This meteorologist is using computers to follow and predict the movement of a powerful storm.

Meteorology
Have you ever seen the [weather on] television? If so, you ha[ve seen the work] of another branch [of geography. This] branch is called **meteorology**, the study of weather and what causes it.

Meteorologists study weather patterns in a particular area. Then they use the information to predict what the weather will be like in the coming days. Their work helps people plan what to wear and what to do on any given day. At the same time, their work can save lives by predicting the arrival of terrible storms. These predictions are among the most visible ways in which the work of geographers affects our lives every day.

READING CHECK **Finding Main Ideas** What are some major branches of geography?

SUMMARY AND PREVIEW In this section, you learned about two main branches of geography, physical and human. In the next chapter, you will learn more about the physical features that surround us and the processes that create them.

Hydrology
Another important branch of geography is hydrology, the study of water on Earth. Geographers in this field study the world's river systems and rainfall patterns. They study what causes droughts and floods and how people in cities can get safe drinking water. They also work to measure and protect the world's supply of water.

FOCUS ON READING
What do you already know about drinking water?

Section 3 Assessment

hmhsocialstudies.com
ONLINE QUIZ

Reviewing Ideas, Terms, and Places
1. a. **Define** What is **physical geography**?
   b. **Explain** Why do we study physical geography?
2. a. **Identify** What are some things that people study as part of **human geography**?
   b. **Summarize** What are some ways in which the study of human geography can influence our lives?
   c. **Evaluate** Which do you think would be more interesting to study, physical geography or human geography? Why?
3. a. **Identify** What are two specialized fields of geography?
   b. **Analyze** How do cartographers contribute to the work of other geographers?

Critical Thinking
4. **Comparing and Contrasting** Draw a diagram like the one shown here. In the left circle, list three features of physical geography from your notes. In the right circle, list three features of human geography. Where the circles overlap, list one feature they share.

Physical   Human

FOCUS ON WRITING
5. **Choosing a Branch** Your job description should point out to people that there are many branches of geography. How will you note that?

20 CHAPTER 1

Reading Check Questions end each section of content so you can check to make sure you understand what you just studied.

Summary and Preview The Summary and Preview connects what you studied in the section to what you will study in the next section.

Section Assessment Finally, the section assessment boxes make sure that you understand the main ideas of the section. We also provide assessment practice online!

Scavenger Hunt

Are you ready to explore the world of geography? **Holt McDougal: Introduction to Geography** is your ticket to this exciting world. Before you begin your journey, complete this scavenger hunt to get to know your book and discover what's inside.

On a separate sheet of paper, fill in the blanks to complete each sentence below. In each answer, one letter will be in a yellow box. When you have answered every question, copy these letters in order to reveal the answer to the question at the bottom of the page.

1 The third key term listed on page 86 is ▢▢▢▢▢▢▢▢.

2 On page 35, the Main Ideas are followed by The ▢▢▢ Idea. How do the Main Ideas connect to what is covered in this section?

3 The Connecting to Science feature on page 64 is called ▢▢▢▢ Factory.

4 The Close-up feature on page 98 is called A ▢▢▢▢▢▢ Economy. What other Close-up features can you find in the book?

5 In the English and Spanish Glossary, the second word in the definition of *cartography* is ▢▢▢▢▢▢▢.

6 The Reading Social Studies lesson on page 107 is called Using ▢▢▢▢▢ ▢▢▢▢▢▢.

7 The subject of the Writing Workshop on Page 104 is ▢▢▢▢▢▢▢▢▢▢ a Process.

There are about 7 ▢▢▢▢▢▢▢ people in the world today.

Introduction to Geography

Deserts

Huge deserts, such as the Sahara in North Africa, are visible from space and appear yellow and brown.

Oceans

About 71 percent of Earth's surface is covered by vast amounts of salt water, which form the world's oceans.

Introduction to Geography

Explore the Satellite Image
Human-made machines that orbit Earth, called satellites, send back images of our planet like this one. What can you learn about Earth from studying this satellite image?

Frozen Lands

Earth's icy poles are frozen year-round and appear a brilliant white from space. These frozen lands contain much of Earth's freshwater.

665.00'

CHAPTER 1

A Geographer's World

Essential Question How does geography help us understand our world?

What You Will Learn...

In this chapter you will learn about the field of geography, the study of the world's people and places. You will also learn why people study geography and how they organize their studies.

FOCUS ON READING AND WRITING

Using Prior Knowledge Prior knowledge is what you already know about a subject. Before you read a chapter, review the chapter and section titles. Then make a list of what you already know. Later, you can compare your prior knowledge with what you learned from the chapter. **See the lesson, Using Prior Knowledge, on page 106.**

Writing a Job Description Geographers are people who study geography, but what is it exactly that they do? As you read this chapter, you will learn about the work that geographers do. Then you will write a job description that could be included in a career-planning guide.

Studying the World Exploring the world takes people to exciting and interesting places.

HISTORY Satellites

↗ hmhsocialstudies.com VIDEO

ANALYSIS SKILL **ANALYZING VISUALS**

This village is in the country of Nepal. It rests high in the Himalayas, the highest mountains in the world.

What is the land around the village like? How can you tell that people live in this area?

Human Geography Geography is also the study of people. It asks where people live, what they eat, what they wear, and even what kinds of animals they keep.

Physical Geography Geography is the study of the world's land features, such as this windswept rock formation in Arizona.

3

Studying Geography

What You Will Learn...

Main Ideas

1. Geography is the study of the world, its people, and the landscapes they create.
2. Geographers look at the world in many different ways.
3. Maps and other tools help geographers study the planet.

The Big Idea

The study of geography and the use of geographic tools helps us view the world in new ways.

Key Terms

geography, *p. 4*
landscape, *p. 4*
social science, *p. 5*
region, *p. 6*
map, *p. 8*
globe, *p. 8*

hmhsocialstudies.com
TAKING NOTES

Use the graphic organizer online to record details about geography and what geographers do.

If YOU lived there...

You have just moved to Miami, Florida, from your old home in Pennsylvania. Everything seems very different—from the weather and the trees to the way people dress and talk. Even the streets and buildings look different. One day you get an e-mail from a friend at your old school. "What's it like living there?" he asks.

How will you describe your new home?

BUILDING BACKGROUND Often, when you are telling someone about a place they have never been, what you are describing is the place's geography. What the place looks like, what kind of weather it has, and how people live there are all parts of its geography.

What Is Geography?

Think about the place where you live. What does the land look like? Are there tall mountains nearby, or is the land so flat that you can see for miles? Is the ground covered with bright green grass and trees, or is the area part of a sandy desert?

Now think about the weather in your area. What is it like? Does it get really hot in the summer? Do you see snow every winter? How much does it rain? Do tornadoes ever strike?

Finally, think about the people who live in your town or city. Do they live mostly in apartments or houses? Do most people own cars, or do they get around town on buses or trains? What kinds of jobs do adults in your town have? Were most of the people you know born in your town, or did they move there?

The things that you have been thinking about are part of your area's geography. **Geography** is the study of the world, its people, and the landscapes they create. To a geographer, a place's **landscape** is all the human and physical features that make it unique. When they study the world's landscapes, geographers ask questions much like the ones you just asked yourself.

Geography as a Science

Many of the questions that geographers ask deal with how the world works. They want to know what causes mountains to form and what creates tornadoes. To answer questions like these, geographers have to think and act like scientists.

As scientists, geographers look at data, or information, that they gather about places. Gathering data can sometimes lead geographers to fascinating places. They might have to crawl deep into caves or climb tall mountains to make observations and take measurements. At other times, geographers study sets of images collected by satellites orbiting high above Earth.

However geographers gather their data, they have to study it carefully. Like other scientists, geographers must examine their findings in great detail before they can learn what all the information means.

Geography as a Social Science

Not everything that geographers study can be measured in numbers, however. Some geographers study people and their lives. For example, they may ask why countries change their governments or why people in a place speak a certain language. This kind of information cannot be measured.

Because it deals with people and how they live, geography is sometimes called a social science. A **social science** is a field that studies people and the relationships among them.

The geographers who study people do not dig in caves or climb mountains. Instead, they visit places and talk to the people who live there. They want to learn about people's lives and communities.

READING CHECK **Analyzing** In what ways is geography both a science and a social science?

What Is Geography?

Geography is the study of the world, its people, and the landscapes they create. To study a place's geography, we look at its physical and human features.

The physical features of Algeria include huge deserts full of tall sand dunes.

Many Algerians live in small villages like this one. The village is one of Algeria's human features.

Together, Algeria's physical and human features create the country's landscape.

ANALYSIS SKILL **ANALYZING VISUALS**

What is the landscape of this part of Algeria like?

Looking at the World

Whether they study volcanoes and storms or people and cities, geographers have to look carefully at the world around them. To fully understand how the world works, geographers often look at places at three different levels.

Local Level

Some geographers study issues at a local level. They ask the same types of questions we asked at the beginning of this chapter: How do people in a town or community live? What is the local government like? How do the people who live there get around? What do they eat?

By asking these questions, geographers can figure out why people live and work the way they do. They can also help people improve their lives. For example, they can help town leaders figure out the best place to build new schools, shopping centers, or sports complexes. They can also help the people who live in the city or town plan for future changes.

Regional Level

Sometimes, though, geographers want to study a bigger chunk of the world. To do this, they divide the world into regions. A **region** is a part of the world that has one or more common features that distinguish it from surrounding areas.

Some regions are defined by physical characteristics such as mountain ranges, climates, or plants native to the area. As a result, these types of regions are often easy to identify. The Rocky Mountains of the western United States, for example, make up a physical region. Another example of this kind of region is the Sahara, a huge desert in northern Africa.

Other regions may not be so easy to define, however. These regions are based on the human characteristics of a place, such as language, religion, or history. A place in which most people share these kinds of characteristics can also be seen as a region. For example, most people in Scandinavia, a region in northern Europe, speak similar languages and practice the same religion.

Looking at the World

Geographers look at the world at many levels. At each level, they ask different questions and discover different types of information. By putting information gathered at different levels together, geographers can better understand a place and its role in the world.

ANALYZING VISUALS Based on these photos, what are some questions a geographer might ask about London?

Local Level This busy neighborhood in London, England, is a local area. A geographer here might study local foods, housing, or clothing.

Regions come in all shapes and sizes. Some are small, like the neighborhood called Chinatown in San Francisco. Other regions are huge, like the Americas. This huge region includes two continents, North America and South America. The size of the area does not matter, as long as the area shares some characteristics. These shared characteristics define the region.

Geographers divide the world into regions for many reasons. The world is a huge place and home to billions of people. Studying so large an area can be extremely difficult. Dividing the world into regions makes it easier to study. A small area is much easier to examine than a large area.

Other geographers study regions to see how people interact with one another. For example, they may study a city such as London, England, to learn how the city's people govern themselves. Then they can compare what they learn about one region to what they learn about another region. In this way, they can learn more about life and landscapes in both places.

Global Level

Sometimes geographers do not want to study the world just at a regional level. Instead they want to learn how people interact globally, or around the world. To do so, geographers ask how events and ideas from one region of the world affect people in other regions. In other words, they study the world on a global level.

Geographers who study the world on a global level try to find relationships among people who live far apart. They may, for example, examine the products that a country exports to see how those products are used in other countries.

In recent decades, worldwide trade and communication have increased. As a result, we need to understand how our actions affect people around the world. Through their studies, geographers provide us with information that helps us figure out how to live in a rapidly changing world.

READING CHECK **Finding Main Ideas** At what levels do geographers study the world?

Regional Level As a major city, London is also a region. At this level, a geographer might study the city's population or transportation systems.

Global Level London is one of the world's main financial centers. Here a geographer might study how London's economy affects the world.

Geographers use many tools to study the world. Each tool provides part of the information a geographer needs to learn what a place is like.

ANALYZING VISUALS What information could you learn from each of these tools?

High School Soccer Participation

Participation in High School Soccer

- More than 9%
- 5–9%
- 3–5%
- Fewer than 3%
- Data not available

Maps usually give geographers more information about a place than globes do. This map, for example, shows rates of soccer participation in the United States.

A geographer can use a globe to see where a place, such as the United States, is located.

The Geographer's Tools

Have you ever seen a carpenter building or repairing a house? If so, you know that builders need many tools to do their jobs correctly. In the same way, geographers need many tools to study the world.

Maps and Globes

FOCUS ON READING
What do you already know about maps and globes?

The tools that geographers use most often in their work are maps and globes. A **map** is a flat drawing that shows all or part of Earth's surface. A **globe** is a spherical, or ball-shaped, model of the entire planet.

Both maps and globes show what the world looks like. They can show where mountains, deserts, and oceans are. They can also identify and describe the world's countries and major cities.

There are, however, major differences between maps and globes. Because a globe is spherical like Earth, it can show the world as it really is.

A map, though, is flat. It is not possible to show a spherical area perfectly on a flat surface. To understand what this means, think about an orange. If you took the peel off of an orange, could you make it lie completely flat? No, you could not, unless you stretched or tore the peel first.

The same principle is true with maps. To draw Earth on a flat surface, people have to distort, or alter, some details. For example, places on a map might look to be farther apart than they really are, or their shapes or sizes might be changed slightly.

Still, maps have many advantages over globes. Flat maps are easier to work with than globes. Also, it is easier to show small areas like cities on maps than on globes.

In addition, maps usually show more information than globes. Because globes are more expensive to make, they do not usually show anything more than where places are and what features they have.

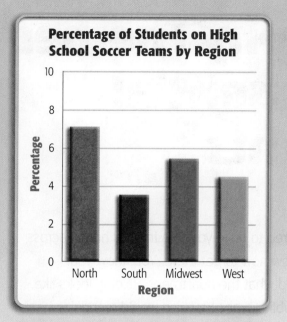

Percentage of Students on High School Soccer Teams by Region

Charts and graphs are also tools geographers can use to study information. They are often used when geographers want to compare numbers, such as the number of students who play soccer in each region of the country.

Maps, on the other hand, can show all sorts of information. Besides showing land use and cities, maps can include a great deal of information about a place. A map might show what languages people speak or where their ancestors came from. Maps like the one on the opposite page can even show how many students in an area play soccer.

Satellite Images

Maps and globes are not the only tools that geographers use in their work. As you have already read, many geographers study information gathered by satellites.

Much of the information gathered by these satellites is in the form of images. Geographers can study these images to see what an area looks like from above Earth. Satellites also collect information that we cannot see from the planet's surface. The information gathered by satellites helps geographers make accurate maps.

Other Tools

Geographers also use many other tools. For example, they use computer programs to create, update, and compare maps. They also use measuring devices to record data. In some cases, the best tools a geographer can use are a notebook and tape recorder to take notes while talking to people. Armed with the proper tools, geographers learn about the world's people and places.

READING CHECK **Summarizing** What are some of the geographer's basic tools?

SUMMARY AND PREVIEW Geography is the study of the world, its people, and its landscapes. In the next section, you will learn about two systems geographers use to organize their studies.

Section 1 Assessment

hmhsocialstudies.com
ONLINE QUIZ

Reviewing Ideas, Terms, and Places

1. **a. Define** What is **geography**?
   b. Explain Why is geography considered a science?
2. **a. Identify** What is a **region**? Give two examples.
   b. Elaborate What global issues do geographers study?
3. **a. Describe** How do geographers use satellite images?
   b. Compare and Contrast How are maps and globes similar? How are they different?

Critical Thinking

4. **Summarizing** Draw three ovals like the ones shown here. Use your notes to fill the ovals with information about geography, geographers, and their tools.

What Geography Is → What Geographers Study → The Geographer's Tools

FOCUS ON WRITING

5. **Describing a Field** Based on what you have learned, what might attract people to work in geography? In your notebook, list some details about geography that might make people interested in working in the field.

Geography Themes and Essential Elements

What You Will Learn...

Main Ideas

1. The five themes of geography help us organize our studies of the world.
2. The six essential elements of geography highlight some of the subject's most important ideas.

The Big Idea

Geographers have created two different but related systems for organizing geographic studies.

Key Terms

absolute location, *p. 12*
relative location, *p. 12*
environment, *p. 12*

hmhsocialstudies.com
TAKING NOTES

Use the graphic organizer online to take notes on the five themes and six essential elements of geography.

If **YOU** lived there...

Your older sister has offered to drive you to a friend's house across town, but she doesn't know how to get there. You know your friend's street address and what the apartment building looks like. You know it's near the public library. You also would recognize some landmarks in the neighborhood, such as the video store and the supermarket.

What might help your sister find the house?

BUILDING BACKGROUND Like drivers, geographers have to know where places are in order to study them. An area's location is only one of the aspects that geographers study, though. In fact, it is only one of the five themes that geographers use to describe a place.

The Five Themes of Geography

Have you ever gone to a Fourth of July party with a patriotic theme? If so, you probably noticed that almost everything at the party was related to that theme. For example, you may have seen American flags and decorations based on the flag's stars and stripes. You may have seen clothes that were red, white, and blue or heard patriotic music being played. Chances are that almost everything at the party reflected the theme of patriotism.

Like party planners, geographers use themes in their work. Geographers do not study parties, of course, but they do note common themes in their studies. Just as a party's theme is reflected in nearly every aspect of the party, these geography themes can be applied to nearly everything that geographers study. The five major themes of geography are Location, Place, Human-Environment Interaction, Movement, and Regions.

The Five Themes of Geography

Geographers use five major themes, or ideas, to organize and guide their studies.

Location The theme of location describes where something is. The mountain shown above, Mount Rainier, is in west-central Washington.

Place Place describes the features that make a site unique. For example, Washington, D.C., is our nation's capital and has many great monuments.

UNITED STATES

Regions Regions are areas that share common characteristics. The Mojave Desert, shown here, is defined by its distinctive climate and plant life.

Movement This theme looks at how and why people and things move. Airports like this one in Dallas, Texas, help people move around the world.

Human-Environment Interaction People interact with their environments in many ways. Some, like this man in Florida, use the land to grow crops.

ANALYSIS SKILL **ANALYZING VISUALS**

Which of the five themes deals with the relationships between people and their surroundings?

Location

Every point on Earth has a location, a description of where it is. This location can be expressed in many ways. Sometimes a site's location is expressed in specific, or absolute, terms, such as an address. For example, the White House is located at 1600 Pennsylvania Avenue in the city of Washington, D.C. A specific description like this one is called an **absolute location**. Other times, the site's location is expressed in general terms. For example, Canada is north of the United States. This general description of where a place lies is called its **relative location**.

Place

Another theme, Place, is closely related to Location. However, Place does not refer simply to where an area is. It refers to the area's landscape, the features that define the area and make it different from other places. Such features could include land, climate, and people. Together, they give a place its own character.

Human-Environment Interaction

FOCUS ON
READING
What do you
know about
environments?

In addition to looking at the features of places, geographers examine how those features interact. In particular, they want to understand how people interact with their environment—how people and their physical environment affect each other. An area's **environment** includes its land, water, climate, plants, and animals.

People interact with their environment every day in all sorts of ways. They clear forests to plant crops, level fields to build cities, and dam rivers to prevent floods. At the same time, physical environments affect how people live. People in cold areas, for example, build houses with thick walls and wear heavy clothing to keep warm. People who live near oceans look for ways to protect themselves from storms.

Movement

People are constantly moving. They move within cities, between cities, and between countries. Geographers want to know why and how people move. For example, they ask if people are moving to find work or to live in a more pleasant area. Geographers also study the roads and routes that make movement so common.

Regions

You have already learned how geographers divide the world into many regions to help the study of geography. Creating regions also makes it easier to compare places. Comparisons help geographers learn why each place has developed the way it has.

READING CHECK **Finding Main Ideas** What are the five themes of geography?

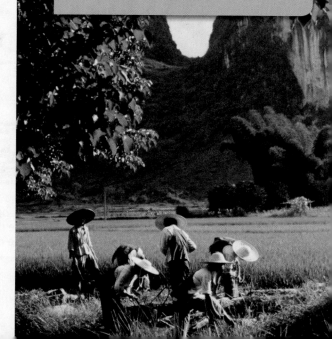

The six essential elements are used by geographers to organize their studies and are closely related to the geography standards. Each element includes several of the standards, as listed in the chart.

ANALYZING VISUALS How many of the six essential elements can you see illustrated in this photo?

The Six Essential Elements

The five themes of geography are not the only system geographers use to study the world. They also use a system of standards and essential **elements**. Together, these standards and essential elements identify the most important ideas in the study of geography. These ideas are expressed in two lists.

The first list is the national geography standards. This is a list of 18 basic ideas that are central to the study of geography. These standards are listed in black type on the chart below.

The essential elements are based on the geography standards. Each element is a big idea that links several standards together. The six essential elements are The World in Spatial Terms, Places and Regions, Physical Systems, Human Systems, Environment and Society, and The Uses of Geography. On the chart, they are shown in purple.

Read through that list again. Do you see any similarities between geography's six essential elements and its five themes? You probably do. The two systems are very similar because the six essential elements build on the five themes.

ACADEMIC VOCABULARY
element part

The Essential Elements and Geography Standards

The World in Spatial Terms

- How to use maps and other geographic representations, tools, and technologies to acquire, process, and report information from a spatial perspective
- How to use mental maps to organize information about people, places, and environments in a spatial context
- How to analyze the spatial organization of people, places, and environments on Earth's surface

Places and Regions

- The physical and human characteristics of places
- How people create regions to interpret Earth's complexity
- How culture and experience influence people's perceptions of places and regions

Physical Systems

- The physical processes that shape the patterns of Earth's surface
- The characteristics and spatial distribution of ecosystems on Earth's surface

Human Systems

- The characteristics, distributions, and migration of human populations on Earth's surface
- The characteristics, distribution, and complexity of Earth's cultural mosaics
- The patterns and networks of economic interdependence on Earth's surface
- The processes, patterns, and functions of human settlement
- How the forces of cooperation and conflict among people influence the division and control of Earth's surface

Environment and Society

- How human actions modify the physical environment
- How physical systems affect human systems
- Changes that occur in the meaning, use, distribution, and importance of resources

The Uses of Geography

- How to apply geography to interpret the past
- How to apply geography to interpret the present and plan for the future

BOOK
Geography for Life

The six essential elements were first outlined in a book called Geography for Life. *In that book, the authors—a diverse group of geographers and teachers from around the United States—explained why the study of geography is important.*

❝Geography *is* for life in every sense of that expression: lifelong, life-sustaining, and life-enhancing. Geography is a field of study that enables us to find answers to questions about the world around us—about where things are and how and why they got there.❞

❝Geography focuses attention on exciting and interesting things, on fascinating people and places, on things worth knowing because they are absorbing and because knowing about them lets humans make better-informed and, therefore, wiser decisions.❞

❝With a strong grasp of geography, people are better equipped to solve issues at not only the local level but also the global level.❞

–from *Geography for Life*,
by the Geography Education Standards Project

ANALYSIS SKILL **ANALYZING PRIMARY SOURCES**

Why do the authors of these passages think that people should study geography?

For example, the element Places and Regions combines two of the five themes of geography—Place and Regions. Also, the element called Environment and Society deals with many of the same issues as the theme Human-Environment Interaction.

There are also some basic differences between the essential elements and the themes. For example, the last element, The Uses of Geography, deals with issues not covered in the five themes. This element examines how people can use geography to plan the landscapes in which they live.

Throughout this book, you will notice references to both the themes and the essential elements. As you read, use these themes and elements to help you organize your own study of geography.

READING CHECK **Summarizing** What are the six essential elements of geography?

SUMMARY AND PREVIEW You have just learned about the themes and elements of geography. Next, you will explore the branches into which the field is divided.

Section 2 Assessment

hmhsocialstudies.com
ONLINE QUIZ

Reviewing Ideas, Terms, and Places

1. **a. Define** What is the difference between a place's **absolute location** and its **relative location**? Give one example of each type of location.
   b. Contrast How are the themes of Location and Place different?
   c. Elaborate How does using the five themes help geographers understand the places they study?
2. **a. Identify** Which of the five themes of geography is associated with airports, highways, and the migration of people from one place to another?
   b. Explain How are the geography standards and the six essential elements related?
   c. Compare How are the six essential elements similar to the five themes of geography?

Critical Thinking

3. **Categorizing** Draw a chart like the one below. Use your notes to list the five themes of geography, explain each of the themes, and list one feature of your city or town that relates to each.

Theme				
Explanation				
Feature				

FOCUS ON WRITING

4. **Including Themes and Essential Elements** The five themes and six essential elements are central to a geographer's job. How will you mention them in your job description? Write down some ideas.

Analyzing Satellite Images

Learn

In addition to maps and globes, satellite images are among the geographer's most valuable tools. Geographers use two basic types of these images. The first type is called true color. These images are like photographs taken from high above Earth's surface. The colors in these images are similar to what you would see from the ground. Vegetation, for example, appears green.

The other type of satellite image is called an infrared image. Infrared images are taken using a special type of light. These images are based on heat patterns, and so the colors on them are not what we might expect. Bodies of water appear black, for example, since they give off little heat.

Practice

Use the satellite images on this page to answer the following questions.

❶ On which image is vegetation red?

❷ Which image do you think probably looks more like Italy does from the ground?

Vegetation appears green.

Water appears blue.

True color satellite image of Italy

Vegetation appears red.

Water appears black.

Infrared satellite image of Italy

Apply

Search the Internet to find a satellite image of your state or region. Determine whether the image is true color or infrared. Then write three statements that describe what you see on the image.

The Branches of Geography

What You Will Learn...

Main Ideas

1. Physical geography is the study of landforms, water bodies, and other physical features.
2. Human geography focuses on people, their cultures, and the landscapes they create.
3. Other branches of geography examine specific aspects of the physical or human world.

The Big Idea

Geography is divided into two main branches—physical and human geography.

Key Terms

physical geography, *p. 16*
human geography, *p. 18*
cartography, *p. 19*
meteorology, *p. 20*

hmhsocialstudies.com
TAKING NOTES

Use the graphic organizer online to take notes on the branches of geography.

If YOU lived there...

You are talking to two friends about the vacations their families will take this summer. One friend says that his family is going to the Grand Canyon. He is very excited about seeing the spectacular landscapes in and around the canyon. Your other friend's family is going to visit Nashville, Tennessee. She is looking forward to trying new foods at the city's restaurants and touring its museums.

Which vacation sounds more interesting? Why?

BUILDING BACKGROUND Geography is the study of the world and its features. Some features are physical, like the Grand Canyon. Others are human, like restaurants and museums. The main branches of geography focus on these types of features.

Physical Geography

Think about a jigsaw puzzle. Seen as a whole, the puzzle shows a pretty or interesting picture. To see that picture, though, you have to put all the puzzle pieces together. Before you assemble them, the pieces do not give you a clear idea of what the puzzle will look like when it is assembled. After all, each piece contains only a tiny portion of the overall image.

In many ways, geography is like a huge puzzle. It is made up of many branches, or divisions. Each of these branches focuses on a single part of the world. Viewed separately, none of these branches shows us the whole world. Together, however, the many branches of geography improve our understanding of our planet and its people.

Geography's two main branches are physical geography and human geography. The first branch, **physical geography**, is the study of the world's physical features—its landforms, bodies of water, climates, soils, and plants. Every place in the world has its own unique combination of these features.

Physical Geography

The study of Earth's physical features, including rivers, mountains, oceans, weather, and other features, such as Victoria Falls in southern Africa

Human Geography

The study of Earth's people, including their ways of life, homes, cities, beliefs, and customs, like those of these children in Malawi, a country in central Africa

Geography

The study of Earth's physical and cultural features

The Physical World

What does it mean to say that physical geography is the study of physical features? Physical geographers want to know all about the different features found on our planet. They want to know where plains and mountain ranges are, how rivers flow across the landscape, and why different amounts of rain fall from place to place.

More importantly, however, physical geographers want to know what causes the different shapes on Earth. They want to know why mountain ranges rise up where they do and what causes rivers to flow in certain directions. They also want to know why various parts of the world have very different weather and climate patterns.

To answer these questions, physical geographers take detailed measurements. They study the heights of mountains and the temperatures of places. To track any changes that occur over time, physical geographers keep careful records of all the information they collect.

Uses of Physical Geography

Earth is made up of hundreds of types of physical features. Without a complete understanding of what these features are and the effect they have on the world's people and landscapes, we cannot fully understand our world. This is the major reason that geographers study the physical world—to learn how it works.

There are also other, more specific reasons for studying physical geography, though. Studying the changes that take place on our planet can help us prepare to live with those changes. For example, knowing what causes volcanoes to erupt can help us predict eruptions. Knowing what causes terrible storms can help us prepare for them. In this way, the work of physical geographers helps us adjust to the dangers and changes of our world.

READING CHECK **Analyzing** What are some features in your area that a physical geographer might study?

Eratosthenes
(c. 276–c. 194 BC)

Did you know that geography is over 2,000 years old? Actually, the study of the world is even older than that, but the first person ever to use the word *geography* lived then. His name was Eratosthenes (er-uh-TAHS-thuh-neez), and he was a Greek scientist and librarian. With no modern instruments of any kind, Eratosthenes figured out how large Earth is. He also drew a map that showed all of the lands that the Greeks knew about. Because of his many contributions to the field, Eratosthenes has been called the Father of Geography.

Generalizing Why is Eratosthenes called the Father of Geography?

Human Geography

The physical world is only one part of the puzzle of geography. People are also part of the world. **Human geography** is the study of the world's people, communities, and landscapes. It is the second major branch of geography.

The Human World

Put simply, human geographers study the world's people, past and present. They look at where people live and why. They ask why some parts of the world have more people than others, and why some places have almost no people at all.

Human geographers also study what people do. What jobs do people have? What crops do they grow? What makes them move from place to place? These are the types of questions that geographers ask about people around the world.

Because people's lives are so different around the world, no one can study every aspect of human geography. As a result, human geographers often specialize in a smaller area of study. Some may choose to study only the people and landscapes in a certain region. For example, a geographer may study only the lives of people who live in West Africa.

Other geographers choose not to limit their studies to one place. Instead, they may choose to examine only one aspect of people's lives. For example, a geographer could study only economics, politics, or city life. However, that geographer may compare economic patterns in various parts of the world to see how they differ.

Uses of Human Geography

Although every culture is different, people around the world have some common needs. All people need food and water. All people need shelter. All people need to deal with other people in order to survive.

Human geographers study how people in various places address their needs. They look at the foods people eat and the types of governments they form. The knowledge they gather can help us better understand people in other cultures. Sometimes this type of understanding can help people improve their landscapes and situations.

On a smaller scale, human geographers can help people design their cities and towns. By understanding where people go and what they need, geographers can help city planners place roads, shopping malls, and schools. Geographers also study the effect people have on the world. As a result, they often work with private groups and government agencies who want to protect the environment.

READING CHECK **Summarizing** What do human geographers study?

Other Fields of Geography

Physical geography and human geography are the two largest branches of the subject, but they are not the only ones. Many other fields of geography exist, each one devoted to studying one aspect of the world.

Most of these fields are smaller, more specialized areas of either physical or human geography. For example, economic geography—the study of how people make and spend money—is a branch of human geography. Another specialized branch of human geography is urban geography, the study of cities and how people live in them. Physical geography also includes many fields, such as the study of climates. Other fields of physical geography are the studies of soils and plants.

Cartography

One key field of geography is **cartography**, the science of making maps. You have already seen how important maps are to the study of geography. Without maps, geographers would not be able to study where things are in the world.

In the past, maps were always drawn by hand. Many were not very accurate. Today, though, most maps are made using computers and satellite images. Through advances in mapmaking, we can make accurate maps on almost any scale, from the whole world to a single neighborhood, and keep them up to date. These maps are not only used by geographers. For example, road maps are used by people who are planning long trips.

CONNECTING TO Technology

Computer Mapping

In the past, maps were drawn by hand. Making a map was a slow process. Even the simplest map took a long time to make. Today, however, cartographers have access to tools people in the past—even people who lived just 50 years ago—never imagined. The most important of these tools are computers.

Computers allow us to make maps quickly and easily. In addition, they let us make new types of maps that people could not make in the past.

The map shown here, for example, was drawn on a computer. It shows the number of computer users in the United States who were connected to the Internet on a particular day. Each of the lines that rises off of the map represents a city in which people were using the Internet. The color of the line indicates the number of computer users in that city. As you can see, this data resulted in a very complex map.

Making such a map required cartographers to sort through huge amounts of complex data. Such sorting would not have been possible without computers.

Contrasting How are today's maps different from those created in the past?

Meteorology is the study of weather. This meteorologist is using computers to follow and predict the movement of a powerful storm.

Meteorology

Have you ever seen the weather report on television? If so, you have seen the results of another branch of geography. This branch is called **meteorology**, the study of weather and what causes it.

Meteorologists study weather patterns in a particular area. Then they use the information to predict what the weather will be like in the coming days. Their work helps people plan what to wear and what to do on any given day. At the same time, their work can save lives by predicting the arrival of terrible storms. These predictions are among the most visible ways in which the work of geographers affects our lives every day.

READING CHECK **Finding Main Ideas** What are some major branches of geography?

SUMMARY AND PREVIEW In this section, you learned about two main branches of geography, physical and human. In the next chapter, you will learn more about the physical features that surround us and the processes that create them.

Hydrology

Another important branch of geography is hydrology, the study of water on Earth. Geographers in this field study the world's river systems and rainfall patterns. They study what causes droughts and floods and how people in cities can get safe drinking water. They also work to measure and protect the world's supply of water.

FOCUS ON READING
What do you already know about drinking water?

Section 3 Assessment

hmhsocialstudies.com
ONLINE QUIZ

Reviewing Ideas, Terms, and Places

1. **a. Define** What is **physical geography**?
   b. Explain Why do we study physical geography?
2. **a. Identify** What are some things that people study as part of **human geography**?
   b. Summarize What are some ways in which the study of human geography can influence our lives?
   c. Evaluate Which do you think would be more interesting to study, physical geography or human geography? Why?
3. **a. Identify** What are two specialized fields of geography?
   b. Analyze How do cartographers contribute to the work of other geographers?

Critical Thinking

4. **Comparing and Contrasting** Draw a diagram like the one shown here. In the left circle, list three features of physical geography from your notes. In the right circle, list three features of human geography. Where the circles overlap, list one feature they share.

   Physical   Human

FOCUS ON WRITING

5. **Choosing a Branch** Your job description should point out to people that there are many branches of geography. How will you note that?

Visual Summary

Use the visual summary below to help you review the main ideas of the chapter.

QUICK FACTS

Physical geography—the study of the world's physical features—is one main branch of geography.

Human geography—the study of the world's people and how they live—is the second main branch.

Geographers use many tools to study the world. The most valuable of these tools are maps.

Reviewing Vocabulary, Terms, and Places

Match the words in the columns with the correct definitions listed below.

1. geography
2. physical geography
3. human geography
4. element
5. meteorology
6. region
7. cartography
8. map
9. landscape
10. globe

a. a part of the world that has one or more common features that make it different from surrounding areas

b. a flat drawing of part of Earth's surface

c. a part

d. a spherical model of the planet

e. the study of the world's physical features

f. the study of weather and what causes it

g. the study of the world, its people, and the landscapes they create

h. the science of making maps

i. the physical and human features that define an area and make it different from other places

j. the study of people and communities

Comprehension and Critical Thinking

SECTION 1 *(Pages 4–9)*

11. a. Identify What are three levels at which a geographer might study the world? Which of these levels covers the largest area?

b. Compare and Contrast How are maps and globes similar? How are they different?

c. Elaborate How might satellite images and computers help geographers improve their knowledge of the world?

SECTION 2 *(Pages 10–14)*

12. a. Define What do geographers mean when they discuss an area's landscape?

b. Explain Why did geographers create the five themes and the six essential elements?

c. Predict How might the five themes and six essential elements help you in your study of geography?

SECTION 3 *(Pages 16–20)*

13. a. Identify What are the two main branches of geography? What does each include?

b. Summarize How can physical geography help people adjust to the dangers of the world?

c. Elaborate Why do geographers study both physical and human characteristics of places?

Using the Internet 21ST CENTURY

14. Activity: Using Maps Through your online textbook, explore how maps can help you understand your community and learn about its features. Then search the Internet to find a map of your community. Use the map to find the locations of at least five important features. For example, you might locate your school, the library, a park, or major highways. Be creative and find other places you think your classmates should be aware of.

🗗 hmhsocialstudies.com

Social Studies Skills

Analyzing Satellite Images *Use the satellite images of Italy from the Social Studies Skills lesson in this chapter to answer the following questions.*

15. On which image do forests appear more clearly, the true-color or the infrared image?

16. What color do you think represents mountains on the infrared satellite image?

17. Why might geographers use satellite images like these while making maps of Italy?

Map Activity

18. Sketch Map Draw a map of your school and the surrounding neighborhood. Your map should include major features like streets and buildings. Use the map shown here as an example.

FOCUS ON READING AND WRITING

19. Using Prior Knowledge Create a chart with three columns. In the first column, list what you knew about geography before you read the chapter. In the second column, list what you learned in the chapter. In the third column, list questions that you now have about geography.

20. Writing Your Job Description Review your notes on the different jobs geographers do. Then write your job description. You should begin your description by explaining why the job is important. Then identify the job's tasks and responsibilities. Finally, tell what kind of person might do well as a geographer.

Standardized Test Prep

DIRECTIONS: *Read questions 1 through 7 and write the letter of the best response. Then read question 8 and write your own well-constructed response.*

1 **Which of the following subjects would a human geographer study the most?**

A mountains

B populations

C rivers

D volcanoes

2 **The study of weather is called**

A meteorology.

B hydrology.

C social science.

D cartography.

3 **A region is an area that has**

A one or more common features.

B no people living in it.

C few physical features.

D set physical boundaries.

4 **How many essential elements of geography have geographers identified?**

A two

B four

C six

D eight

5 **The physical and human characteristics that define an area are its**

A landscape.

B location.

C region.

D science.

The United States

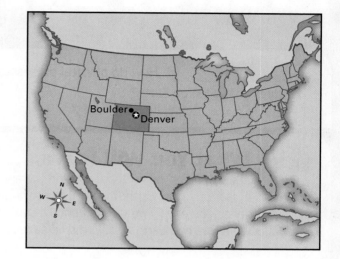

6 **Which of the five themes of geography would a geographer most likely study using this map?**

A movement

B location

C human-environment interaction

D landscape

7 **The smallest level at which a geographer might study a place is**

A microscopic.

B local.

C regional.

D global.

8 **Extended Response** Look at the map of the United States above. Do you think this map is more likely to be used by a physical geographer or by a human geographer? Give two reasons for your answer. Then write two statements about what a geographer could find on this map.

CHAPTER 2

Planet Earth

Essential Question How do physical processes and features shape life on Earth?

 ## What You Will Learn...

In this chapter you will learn about important processes on planet Earth. You will discover how Earth's movements affect the energy we receive from the sun, how water affects life, and how Earth's landforms were made.

FOCUS ON READING AND WRITING

Using Word Parts Sometimes you can figure out the meaning of a word by looking at its parts. A root is the base of the word. A prefix attaches to the beginning, and a suffix attaches to the ending. When you come across a word you don't know, check to see whether you recognize its parts. **See the lesson, Using Word Parts, on page 107.**

Writing a Haiku Join the poets who have celebrated our planet for centuries. Write a haiku, a short poem, about planet Earth. As you read the chapter, gather information about changes in the sun's energy, Earth's water supply, and shapes on the land. Then choose the most intriguing information to include in your haiku.

Energy from the Sun The planet's movement creates differences in the amount of energy Earth receives from the sun.

HISTORY.
How the Earth Was Made

⃠ hmhsocialstudies.com ► VIDEO

ANALYSIS SKILL | ANALYZING VISUALS

Many of Earth's features are visible from space. This photo, taken from a satellite orbiting the planet, shows part of the North American continent.

Which of Earth's features are visible in this photo?

Land Forces on and under Earth's surface have shaped the different landforms on our planet. Geographers study how mountains and other landforms were made.

Water on Earth Water is essential for life on Earth. Much of the planet's water supply is stored in Earth's oceans and ice caps.

Earth and the Sun's Energy

hmhsocialstudies.com
TAKING NOTES

Use the graphic organizer online to take notes on Earth's movement and the seasons.

If YOU lived there...

You live in Chicago and have just won an exciting prize—a trip to Australia during winter vacation in January. As you prepare for the trip, your mother reminds you to pack shorts and a swimsuit. You are confused. In January you usually wear winter sweaters and a heavy jacket.

Why is the weather so different in Australia?

BUILDING BACKGROUND Seasonal differences in weather are an important result of Earth's constant movement. As the planet moves, we experience changes in the amount of energy we receive from the sun. Geographers study and explain why different places on Earth receive differing amounts of energy from the sun.

Earth's Movement

Energy from the sun helps crops grow, provides light, and warms Earth. It even influences the clothes we wear, the foods we eat, and the sports we play. All life on Earth requires **solar energy**, or energy from the sun, to survive. The amount of solar energy places on Earth receive changes constantly. Earth's rotation, revolution, and tilt, as well as latitude, all affect the amount of solar energy parts of the planet receive from the sun.

Rotation

Imagine that Earth has a rod running through it from the North Pole to the South Pole. This rod represents Earth's axis—an imaginary line around which a planet turns. As Earth spins on its axis, different parts of the planet face the sun. It takes Earth 24 hours, or one day, to complete this rotation. A **rotation** is one complete spin of Earth on its axis. As Earth rotates during this 24-hour period, it appears to us that the sun moves across the sky. The sun seems to rise in the east and set in the west. The

Solar Energy

Earth's tilt and rotation cause changes in the amount of energy we receive from the sun. As Earth rotates on its axis, energy from the sun creates periods of day and night. Earth's tilt causes some locations, especially those close to the equator, to receive more direct solar energy than others.

HISTORY VIDEO
Secrets of the Sun

⤴ hmhsocialstudies.com

←23.5°

North Pole

Sun's Rays

Equator

South Pole

ANALYSIS SKILL | ANALYZING VISUALS

Is the region north or south of the equator receiving more solar energy? How can you tell?

sun, however, does not move. It is actually Earth's rotation that creates the sense of the sun's movement.

Earth's rotation also explains why day changes to night. As you can see in the illustration, solar energy strikes only the half of Earth facing the sun. Warmth and light from the sun create daytime. At the same time, the half of the planet facing away from the sun experiences the cooler temperatures and darkness of night. Earth's rotation causes regular shifts from day to night. As a result, levels of solar energy on Earth constantly change.

Revolution

As Earth spins on its axis, it also follows a path, or orbit, around the sun. Earth's orbit around the sun is not a perfect circle. Sometimes the orbit takes Earth closer to the sun, and at other times the orbit takes it farther away. It takes 365¼ days for Earth to complete one **revolution**, or trip around the sun. We base our calendar year on the time it takes Earth to complete its orbit around the sun. To allow for the fraction of a day, we add an extra day—February 29—to our calendar every four years.

Tilt and Latitude

Another **factor** affecting the amount of solar energy we receive is the planet's tilt. As the illustration shows, Earth's axis is not straight up and down. It is actually tilted at an angle of 23½ degrees from vertical. At any given time of year, some locations on Earth are tilting away from the sun, and others are tilting toward it. Places tilting toward the sun receive more solar energy and experience warmer temperatures. Those tilting away from the sun receive less solar energy and experience cooler temperatures.

A location's **latitude**, the distance north or south of Earth's equator, also affects the amount of solar energy it receives. Low-latitude areas, those near the equator like Hawaii, receive direct rays from the sun all year. These direct rays are more intense and produce warmer temperatures. Regions with high latitudes, like Antarctica, are farther from the equator. As a result, they receive indirect rays from the sun and have colder temperatures.

READING CHECK Finding Main Ideas What factors affect the solar energy Earth receives?

ACADEMIC VOCABULARY

factor cause

The Seasons

FOCUS ON READING

The prefix *hemi-* means half. What does the word *hemisphere* mean?

Does the thought of snow in July or 100-degree temperatures in January seem odd to you? It might if you live in the Northern Hemisphere, where cold temperatures are common in January, not July. The planet's changing seasons explain why we often connect certain weather with specific times of the year, like snow in January. Seasons are periods during the year that are known for a particular type of weather. Many places on Earth experience four seasons—winter, spring, summer, and fall. These seasons are based on temperature and length of day. In some parts of the world, however, seasons are based on the amount of rainfall.

Winter and Summer

The change in seasons is created by Earth's tilt. As you can see in the illustration below, while one of Earth's poles tilts away from the sun, the other tilts toward it. During winter part of Earth is tilted away from the sun, causing less direct solar energy, cool temperatures, and less daylight. Summer occurs when part of Earth is tilted toward the sun. This creates more direct solar energy, warmer temperatures, and longer periods of daylight.

Because of Earth's tilt, the Northern and Southern hemispheres experience opposite seasons. As the North Pole tilts toward the sun in summer, the South Pole tilts away

The Seasons: Northern Hemisphere

As Earth orbits the sun, the tilt of its axis toward and away from the sun causes the seasons to change. Seasons in the Northern Hemisphere change at about the same time every year.

ANALYZING VISUALS As the Northern Hemisphere experiences winter, what season is it in the Southern Hemisphere?

March 21 SPRING

Winter and Spring The North Pole tilts away from the sun in winter, causing cooler temperatures. In the spring, temperatures gradually rise as the North Pole begins to point toward the sun.

December 21 WINTER

June 21 SUMMER

Summer and Fall Summer's warm temperatures are the result of the North Pole's tilt toward the sun. As we move away from the sun in the fall, temperatures slowly decline.

North Pole

Tropic of Cancer

Equator

Tropic of Capricorn

South Pole

September 22

from it. As a result, the Southern Hemisphere experiences winter. Likewise, when it is spring in the Northern Hemisphere, it is fall in the Southern Hemisphere.

Spring and Fall

As Earth orbits the sun, there are periods when the poles tilt neither toward nor away from the sun. These periods mark spring and fall. During the spring, as part of Earth begins to tilt toward the sun, solar energy increases. Temperatures slowly start to rise, and days grow longer. In the fall the opposite occurs as winter approaches. Solar energy begins to decrease, causing cooler temperatures and shorter days.

Rainfall and Seasons

Some regions on Earth have seasons marked by rainfall rather than temperature. This is true in the **tropics**, regions close to the equator. At certain times of year, winds bring either dry or moist air to the tropics, creating wet and dry seasons. In India, for example, seasonal winds called monsoons bring heavy rains from June to October and dry air from November to January.

READING CHECK **Identifying Cause and Effect** What causes the seasons to change?

The Midnight Sun

Can you imagine going to sleep late at night with the sun shining in the sky? People who live near the Arctic and Antarctic circles experience this every summer, when they can receive up to 24 hours of sunlight a day. The time-lapse photo below shows a typical sunset during this period—except the sun never really sets! This phenomenon is known as the midnight sun. For locations like Tromso, Norway, this means up to two months of constant daylight each summer. People living near Earth's poles often use the long daylight hours to work on outdoor projects in preparation for winter, when they can receive 24 hours of darkness a day.

Predicting How might people's daily lives be affected by the midnight sun?

SUMMARY AND PREVIEW Solar energy is crucial for all life on the planet. Earth's position and movements affect the amount of energy we receive from the sun and determine our seasons. Next, you will learn about Earth's water supply and its importance to us.

Section 1 Assessment

Reviewing Ideas, Terms, and Places

1. **a. Identify** What is **solar energy**, and how does it affect Earth?
   b. Analyze How do **rotation** and tilt each affect the amount of solar energy that different parts of Earth receive?
   c. Predict What might happen if Earth received less solar energy than it currently does?
2. **a. Describe** Name and describe Earth's seasons.
   b. Contrast How are seasons different in the Northern and Southern hemispheres?
   c. Elaborate How might the seasons affect human activities?

Critical Thinking

3. **Identifying Cause and Effect** Use your notes and the diagram to identify the causes of seasons.

FOCUS ON WRITING

4. **Describing the Seasons** What are the seasons like where you live? In your notebook, jot down a few notes that describe the changing seasons.

Water on Earth

What You Will Learn...

Main Ideas

1. Salt water and freshwater make up Earth's water supply.
2. In the water cycle, water circulates from Earth's surface to the atmosphere and back again.
3. Water plays an important role in people's lives.

The Big Idea

Water is a dominant feature on Earth's surface and is essential for life.

Key Terms

freshwater, *p. 31*
glaciers, *p. 31*
surface water, *p. 31*
precipitation, *p. 31*
groundwater, *p. 32*
water vapor, *p. 32*
water cycle, *p. 33*

hmhsocialstudies.com
TAKING NOTES

Use the graphic organizer online to take notes on Earth's water.

If YOU lived there...

You live in the desert Southwest, where heavy water use and a lack of rainfall have led to water shortages. Your city plans to begin a water conservation program that asks people to limit how much water they use. Many of your neighbors have complained that the program is unnecessary. Others support the plan to save water.

How do you feel about the city's water plan?

BUILDING BACKGROUND Although water covers much of Earth's surface, water shortages, like those in the American Southwest, are common all over the planet. Because water is vital to the survival of all living things, geographers study Earth's water supply.

Earth's Water Supply

Think of the different uses for water. We use water to cook and clean, we drink it, and we grow crops with it. Water is used for recreation, to generate electricity, and even to travel from place to place. Water is perhaps the most important and abundant resource on Earth. In fact, water covers some two-thirds of the planet. Understanding Earth's water supply and how it affects our lives is an important part of geography.

Earth's Distribution of Water

Earth's water supply is divided into two main types—salt water and freshwater. Humans, plants, and animals rely on Earth's freshwater supply for survival.

Salt Water

Although water covers much of the planet, we cannot use most of it. About 97 percent of the Earth's water is salt water. Because salt water contains high levels of salt and other minerals, it is unsafe to drink.

In general, salt water is found in Earth's oceans. Oceans are vast bodies of water covering some 71 percent of the planet's surface. Earth's oceans are made up of smaller bodies of water such as seas, gulfs, bays, and straits. Altogether, Earth's oceans cover some 139 million square miles (360 million square km) of the planet's surface.

Some of Earth's lakes contain salt water. The Great Salt Lake in Utah, for example, is a saltwater lake. As salt and other minerals have collected in the lake, which has no outlet, the water has become salty.

Freshwater

Since the water in Earth's oceans is too salty to use, we must rely on other sources for freshwater. **Freshwater**, or water without salt, makes up only about 3 percent of our total water supply. Much of that freshwater is locked in Earth's **glaciers**, large areas of slow-moving ice, and in the ice of the Antarctic and Arctic regions. Most of the freshwater we use everyday is found in lakes, in rivers, and under Earth's surface.

One form of freshwater is surface water. **Surface water** is water that is found in Earth's streams, rivers, and lakes. It may seem that there is a great deal of water in our lakes and rivers, but only a tiny amount of Earth's water supply—less than 1 percent—comes from surface water.

Streams and rivers are a common source of surface water. Streams form when precipitation collects in a narrow channel and flows toward the ocean. **Precipitation** is water that falls to Earth's surface as rain, snow, sleet, or hail. In turn, streams join together to form rivers. Any smaller stream or river that flows into a larger stream or river is called a tributary. For example, the Missouri River is the largest tributary of the Mississippi River.

Lakes are another important source of surface water. Some lakes were formed as rivers filled low-lying areas with water. Other lakes, like the Great Lakes along the U.S.–Canada border, were formed when glaciers carved deep holes in Earth's surface and deposited water as they melted.

Most of Earth's available freshwater is stored underground. As precipitation falls to Earth, much of it is absorbed into the ground, filling spaces in the soil and rock.

Salt Water Earth's oceans contain some 97 percent of the planet's water supply. Unfortunately, this water is too salty to drink.

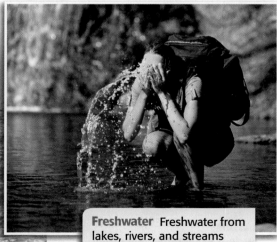

Freshwater Freshwater from lakes, rivers, and streams makes up only a fraction of Earth's water supply.

Water found below Earth's surface is called **groundwater**. In some places on Earth, groundwater naturally bubbles from the ground as a spring. More often, however, people obtain groundwater by digging wells, or deep holes dug into the ground to reach the water.

READING CHECK **Contrasting** How is salt water different from freshwater?

↗ hmhsocialstudies.com **INTERACTIVE ART**
Close-up

The Water Cycle

Energy from the sun drives the water cycle. Surface water evaporates into Earth's atmosphere, where it condenses, then falls back to Earth as precipitation. This cycle repeats continuously, providing us with a fairly constant water supply.

The Water Cycle

When you think of water, you probably visualize a liquid—a flowing stream, a glass of ice-cold water, or a wave hitting the beach. But did you know that water is the only substance on Earth that occurs naturally as a solid, a liquid, and a gas? We see water as a solid in snow and ice and as a liquid in oceans and rivers. Water also occurs in the air as an invisible gas called **water vapor**.

Water is always moving. As water heats up and cools down, it moves from the planet's surface to the atmosphere, or the mass of air that surrounds Earth. One of the most important processes in nature

Condensation occurs when water vapor cools and forms clouds.

When the droplets in clouds become too heavy, they fall to Earth as precipitation.

Runoff is excess precipitation that flows over land into rivers, streams, and oceans.

ANALYSIS SKILL **ANALYZING VISUALS**
How does evaporation differ from precipitation?

is the water cycle. The **water cycle** is the movement of water from Earth's surface to the atmosphere and back.

The sun's energy drives the water cycle. As the sun heats water on Earth's surface, some of that water evaporates, or turns from liquid to gas, or water vapor. Water vapor then rises into the air. As the vapor rises, it cools. The cooling causes the water vapor to condense, or change from a vapor into tiny liquid droplets. These droplets join together to form clouds. If the droplets become heavy enough, precipitation occurs—that is, the water falls back to Earth as rain, snow, sleet, or hail.

When that precipitation falls back to Earth's surface, some of the water is absorbed into the soil as groundwater. Excess water, called runoff, flows over land and collects in streams, rivers, and oceans. Because the water cycle is constantly repeating, it allows us to maintain a fairly constant supply of water on Earth.

READING CHECK **Finding Main Ideas** What is the water cycle?

As energy from the sun heats water on Earth's surface, the water evaporates, or turns to water vapor, and rises to the atmosphere.

Water and People

How many times a day do you think about water? Many of us rarely give it a second thought, yet water is crucial for survival. Water problems such as the lack of water, polluted water, and flooding are concerns for people all around the world. Water also provides us with countless benefits, such as energy and recreation.

Water Problems

One of the greatest water problems people face is a lack of available freshwater. Many places face water shortages as a result of droughts, or long periods of lower-than-normal precipitation. Another cause of water shortages is overuse. In places like the southwestern United States, where the population has grown rapidly, the heavy demand for water has led to shortages.

Even where water is plentiful, it may not be clean enough to use. If chemicals and household wastes make their way into streams and rivers, they can contaminate the water supply. Polluted water can carry diseases. These diseases may harm humans, plants, and animals.

Flooding is another water problem that affects people around the world. Heavy rains often lead to flooding, which can damage property and threaten lives. One example of dangerous flooding occurred in Bangladesh in 2004. Severe floods there destroyed roads and schools, affecting about 25 million people.

Water's Benefits

Water does more than just quench our thirst. It provides us with many benefits, such as food, power, and even recreation.

Water's most important benefit is that it provides us with food to eat. Everything we eat depends on water. For example, fruits and vegetables need water to grow.

FOCUS ON READING
Look at the word *countless* in this paragraph. The suffix *-less* means unable to. What does *countless* mean?

The Benefits of Water

Many people take advantage of the recreational and agricultural benefits that water provides.

Animals also need water to live and grow. As a result, we use water to farm and raise animals so that we will have food to eat.

Water is also an important source of energy. Using dams, we harness the power of moving water to produce electricity. Electricity provides power to air-condition or heat our homes, to run our washers and dryers, and to keep our food cold.

Water also provides us with recreation. Rivers, lakes, and oceans make it possible for us to swim, to fish, to surf, or to sail a boat. Although recreation is not critical for our survival, it does make our lives richer and more enjoyable.

READING CHECK **Summarizing** How does water affect people's lives?

SUMMARY AND PREVIEW In this section you learned that water is essential for life on Earth. Next, you will learn about the shapes on Earth's surface.

Section 2 Assessment

Reviewing Ideas, Terms, and Places

1. **a. Describe** Name and describe the different types of water that make up Earth's water supply.
   b. Analyze Why is only a small percentage of Earth's **freshwater** available to us?
   c. Elaborate In your opinion, which is more important—**surface water** or **groundwater**? Why?
2. **a. Recall** What drives the **water cycle**?
   b. Make Inferences From what bodies of water do you think most evaporation occurs? Why?
3. **a. Define** What is a drought?
   b. Analyze How does water support life on Earth?
   c. Evaluate What water problem do you think is most critical in your community? Why?

Critical Thinking

4. **Sequencing** Draw the graphic organizer at right. Then use your notes and the graphic organizer to identify the stages in Earth's water cycle.

FOCUS ON WRITING

5. **Learning about Water** Consider what you have learned about water in this section. How might you describe water in your haiku? What words might you use to describe Earth's water supply?

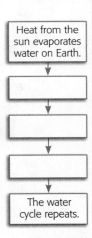

Heat from the sun evaporates water on Earth.

↓

↓

↓

The water cycle repeats.

The Land

If YOU lived there...

You live in the state of Washington. All your life, you have looked out at the beautiful, cone-shaped peaks of nearby mountains. One of them is Mount Saint Helens, an active volcano. You know that in 1980 it erupted violently, blowing a hole in the mountain and throwing ash and rock into the sky. Since then, scientists have watched the mountain carefully.

How do you feel about living near a volcano?

BUILDING BACKGROUND Over billions of years, many different forces have changed Earth's surface. Processes deep underground have built up landforms and even shifted the position of continents. Wind, water, and ice have also shaped the planet's landforms. Changes in Earth's surface continue to take place.

Landforms

Do you know the difference between a valley and a volcano? Can you tell a peninsula from a plateau? If you answered yes, then you are familiar with some of Earth's many landforms. **Landforms** are shapes on the planet's surface, such as hills or mountains. Landforms make up the landscapes that surround us, whether it's the rugged mountains of central Colorado or the flat plains of Oklahoma.

Earth's surface is covered with landforms of many different shapes and sizes. Some important landforms include:

- mountains, land that rises higher than 2,000 feet (610 m)
- valleys, areas of low land located between mountains or hills
- plains, stretches of mostly flat land
- islands, areas of land completely surrounded by water
- peninsulas, land surrounded by water on three sides

Because landforms play an important role in geography, many scientists study how landforms are made and how they affect human activity.

READING CHECK **Summarizing** What are some common landforms?

What You Will Learn...

Main Ideas
1. Earth's surface is covered by many different landforms.
2. Forces below Earth's surface build up our landforms.
3. Forces on the planet's surface shape Earth's landforms.
4. Landforms influence people's lives and culture.

The Big Idea
Processes below and on Earth's surface shape the planet's physical features.

Key Terms
landforms, *p. 35*
continents, *p. 36*
plate tectonics, *p. 36*
lava, *p. 37*
earthquakes, *p. 38*
weathering, *p. 39*
erosion, *p. 39*

hmhsocialstudies.com
TAKING NOTES

Use the graphic organizer online to take notes on Earth's landforms.

Forces below Earth's Surface

Geographers often study how landforms are made. One explanation for how landforms have been shaped involves forces below Earth's surface.

Earth's Plates

ACADEMIC
VOCABULARY

structure the
way something
is set up or
organized

To understand how these forces work, we must examine Earth's **structure**. The planet is made up of three layers. A solid inner core is surrounded by a liquid layer, or mantle. The solid outer layer of Earth is called the crust. The planet's **continents**, or large landmasses, are part of Earth's crust.

Geographers use the theory of plate tectonics to explain how forces below Earth's surface have shaped our landforms. The theory of **plate tectonics** suggests that Earth's surface is divided into a dozen or so slow-moving plates, or pieces of Earth's crust. As you can see in the image below, some plates, like the Pacific plate, are quite large. Others, like the Nazca plate, are much smaller. These plates cover Earth's entire surface. Some plates are under the ocean. These are known as ocean plates. Other plates, known as continental plates, are under Earth's continents.

Why do these plates move? Energy deep inside the planet puts pressure on Earth's crust. As this pressure builds up, it forces the plates to shift. Earth's tectonic plates all move. However, they move in different directions and at different speeds.

The Movement of Continents

Earth's tectonic plates move slowly—up to several inches per year. The continents, which are part of Earth's plates, shift as the plates move. If we could look back some 200 million years, we would see that the continents have traveled great distances. This idea is known as continental drift.

Earth's Plates

hmhsocialstudies.com
ANIMATED GEOGRAPHY

map zone

North American plate

Eurasian plate

Pacific plate

Nazca plate

South American plate

African plate

Indian plate

Australia plate

Antarctic plate

The theory of continental drift, first developed by Alfred Wegener, states that the continents were once united in a single supercontinent. According to this theory, Earth's plates shifted over millions of years. As a result, the continents slowly separated and moved to their present positions.

Earth's continents are still moving. Some plates move toward each other and collide. Other plates separate and move apart. Still others slide past one another. Over time, colliding, separating, and sliding plates have shaped Earth's landforms.

Plates Collide

As plates collide, the energy created from their collision produces distinct landforms. The collision of different types of plates creates different shapes on Earth's surface. Ocean trenches and mountain ranges are two examples of landforms produced by the collision of tectonic plates.

BIOGRAPHY

Alfred Wegener
(1880–1930)

German scientist Alfred Wegener's fascination with the similarities between the western coast of Africa and the eastern coast of South America led to his theory of continental drift. Wegener argued that the two continents had once been joined together. Years of plate movement broke the continents apart and moved them to their current locations. It was only after Wegener's death that his ideas became a central part of the theory of plate tectonics.

The theory of plate tectonics suggests that the plates that make up Earth's crust are moving, usually only a few inches per year. As Earth's plates collide, separate, and slide past each other, they create forces great enough to shape many of Earth's landforms.

ANALYZING VISUALS Looking at the map, what evidence indicates that plates have collided or separated?

When two ocean plates collide, one plate pushes under the other. This process creates ocean trenches. Ocean trenches are deep valleys in the ocean floor. Near Japan, for example, the Pacific plate is slowly moving under other plates. This collision has created several deep ocean trenches, including the world's deepest trench, the Mariana Trench.

Ocean plates and continental plates can also collide. When this occurs, the ocean plate drops beneath the continental plate. This action forces the land above to crumple and form a mountain range. The Andes in South America, for example, were formed when the South American and Nazca plates collided.

The collision of two continental plates also results in mountain-building. When continental plates collide, the land pushes up, sometimes to great heights. The world's highest mountain range, the Himalayas, formed when the Indian plate crashed into the Eurasian plate. In fact, the Himalayas are still growing as the two plates continue to crash into each other.

Plates Separate

A second type of plate movement causes plates to separate. As plates move apart, gaps between the plates allow magma, a liquid rock from the planet's interior, to rise to Earth's crust. **Lava**, or magma that reaches Earth's surface, emerges from the gap that has formed. As the lava cools, it builds a mid-ocean ridge, or underwater mountain. For example, the separation of the North American and Eurasian plates formed the largest underwater mountain, the Mid-Atlantic Ridge. If these mid-ocean ridges grow high enough, they can rise above the surface of the ocean, forming volcanic islands. Iceland, on the boundary of the Eurasian and North American plates, is an example of such an island.

FOCUS ON READING
The suffix –sion means the act of. What does the word collision mean?

Plates Slide

VIDEO
Earthquakes

hmhsocialstudies.com

Tectonic plates also slide past each other. As plates pass by one another, they sometimes grind together. This grinding produces **earthquakes**—sudden, violent movements of Earth's crust. Earthquakes often take place along faults, or breaks in Earth's crust where movement occurs. In California, for example, the Pacific plate is sliding by the edge of the North American plate. This has created the San Andreas Fault zone, an area where earthquakes are quite common.

The San Andreas Fault zone is one of many areas that lie along the boundaries of the Pacific plate. The frequent movement of this plate produces many earthquakes and volcanic eruptions along its edges. In fact, the region around the Pacific plate, called the Ring of Fire, is home to most of the world's earthquakes and volcanoes.

READING CHECK **Finding Main Ideas** What forces below Earth's surface shape landforms?

Plate Movement

The movement of tectonic plates has produced many of Earth's landforms. Volcanoes, islands, and mountains often result from the separation or collision of Earth's plates.

ANALYZING VISUALS What type of landform is created by the collision of two continental plates?

Plate A
Plate B
magma

The separation of plates can allow magma to rise up and create volcanic islands like Surtsey Island, near Iceland.

Plate A
Plate B

The Himalayas in South Asia resulted from the collision of two massive continental plates.

Forces on Earth's Surface

For millions of years, the movement of Earth's tectonic plates has been building up landforms on Earth's surface. At the same time, other forces are working to change those very same landforms.

Imagine a small pile of dirt and rock on a table. If you poured water on the pile, it would move the dirt and rock from one place to another. Likewise, if you were to blow at the pile, the rock and dirt would also move. The same process happens in nature. Weather, water, and other forces change Earth's landforms by wearing them away or reshaping them.

Weathering

One force that wears away landforms is weathering. **Weathering** is the process by which rock is broken down into smaller pieces. Several factors cause rock to break down. In desert areas, daytime heating and nighttime cooling can cause rocks to crack. Water may get into cracks in rocks and freeze. The ice then expands with a force great enough to break the rock. Even the roots of trees can pry rocks apart.

Regardless of which weathering process is at work, rocks eventually break down. These small pieces of rock are known as sediment. Once weathering has taken place, wind, ice, and water often move sediment from one place to another.

Erosion

Another force that changes landforms is the process of erosion. **Erosion** is the movement of sediment from one location to another. Erosion can wear away or build up landforms. Wind, ice, and water all cause erosion.

Powerful winds often cause erosion. Winds lift sediment into the air and carry it across great distances. On beaches and in deserts, wind can deposit large amounts of sand to form dunes. Blowing sand can also wear down rock. The sand acts like sandpaper to polish and wear away at rocks. As you can see in the photo below, wind can have a dramatic effect on landforms.

Earth's glaciers also have the power to cause massive erosion. Glaciers, or large, slow-moving sheets of ice, build up when winter snows do not melt the following summer. Glaciers can be huge. Glaciers in Greenland and Antarctica, for example, are great sheets of ice up to two miles (3 km) thick. Some glaciers flow slowly downhill like rivers of ice. As they do so, they erode the land by carving large U-shaped valleys and sharp mountain peaks. As the ice flows downhill, it crushes rock into sediment and can move huge rocks long distances.

Wind Erosion

Landforms in Utah's Canyonlands National Park have been worn away mostly by thousands of years of powerful winds.

Water is the most common cause of erosion. Waves in oceans and lakes can wear away the shore, creating jagged coastlines, like those on the coast of Oregon. Rivers also cause erosion. Over many years, the flowing water can cut through rock, forming canyons, or narrow areas with steep walls. Arizona's Horseshoe Bend and Grand Canyon are examples of canyons created in this way.

Flowing water shapes other landforms as well. When water deposits sediment in new locations, it creates new landforms. For example, rivers create floodplains when they flood their banks and deposit sediment along the banks. Sediment that is carried by a river all the way out to sea creates a delta. The sediment settles to the bottom, where the river meets the sea. The Nile and Mississippi rivers have created two of the world's largest river deltas.

READING CHECK **Comparing** How are weathering and erosion similar?

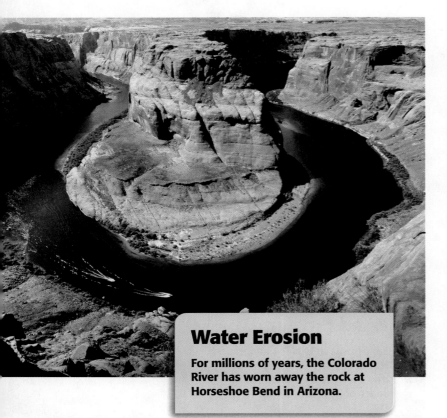

Water Erosion

For millions of years, the Colorado River has worn away the rock at Horseshoe Bend in Arizona.

Landforms Influence Life

Why do you live where you do? Perhaps your family moved to the desert to avoid harsh winter weather. Or possibly one of your ancestors settled near a river delta because its fertile soil was ideal for growing crops. Maybe your family wanted to live near the ocean to start a fishing business. As these examples show, landforms exert a strong influence on people's lives. Earth's landforms affect our settlements and our culture. At the same time, we affect the landforms around us.

Earth's landforms can influence where people settle. People sometimes settle near certain landforms and avoid others. For example, many settlements are built near fertile river valleys or deltas. The earliest urban civilization, for example, was built in the valley between the Tigris and Euphrates rivers. Other times, landforms discourage people from settling in a certain place. Tall, rugged mountains, like the Himalayas, and harsh desert climates, like the Sahara, do not usually attract large settlements.

Landforms affect our culture in ways that we may not have noticed. Landforms often influence what jobs are available in a region. For example, rich mineral deposits in the mountains of Colorado led to the development of a mining industry there. Landforms even affect language. On the island of New Guinea in Southeast Asia, rugged mountains have kept the people so isolated that more than 700 languages are spoken on the island today.

People sometimes change landforms to suit their needs. People may choose to modify landforms in order to improve their lives. For example, engineers built the Panama Canal to make travel from the Atlantic Ocean to the Pacific Ocean easier. In Southeast Asia, people who farm on steep hillsides cut terraces into the slope to

Living with Landforms

The people of Rio de Janeiro, Brazil, have learned to adapt to the mountains and bays that dominate their landscape.

ANALYZING VISUALS How have people in Rio de Janiero adapted to their landscape?

create more level space to grow their crops. People have even built huge dams along rivers to divert water for use in nearby towns or farms.

READING CHECK **Analyzing** What are some examples of humans adjusting to and changing landforms?

SUMMARY AND PREVIEW Landforms are created by actions deep within the planet's surface, and they are changed by forces on Earth's surface, like weathering and erosion. In the next chapter you will learn how other forces, like weather and climate, affect Earth's people.

Section 3 Assessment

Reviewing Ideas, Terms, and Places

1. **a. Describe** What are some common **landforms**?
   b. Analyze Why do geographers study landforms?
2. **a. Identify** What is the theory of **plate tectonics**?
   b. Compare and Contrast How are the effects of colliding plates and separating plates similar and different?
   c. Predict How might Earth's surface change as tectonic plates continue to move?
3. **a. Recall** What is the process of **weathering**?
   b. Elaborate How does water affect sediment?
4. **a. Recall** How do landforms affect life on Earth?
   b. Predict How might people adapt to life in an area with steep mountains?

Critical Thinking

5. **Analyzing** Use your notes and the chart below to identify the different factors that alter Earth's landforms and the changes that they produce.

Factor	Change in Landform

FOCUS ON WRITING

6. **Writing about Earth's Land** Think of some vivid words you could use to describe Earth's landforms. As you think of them, add them to your notebook.

The Ring of Fire

Essential Elements

The World in Spatial Terms
Places and Regions
Physical Systems
Human Systems
Environment and Society
The Uses of Geography

Background Does "the Ring of Fire" sound like the title of a fantasy novel? It's actually the name of a region that circles the Pacific Ocean known for its fiery volcanoes and powerful earthquakes. The Ring of Fire stretches from the tip of South America all the way up to Alaska, and from Japan down to the islands east of Australia. Along this belt, the Pacific plate moves against several other tectonic plates. As a result, thousands of earthquakes occur there every year, and dozens of volcanoes erupt.

The Eruption of Mount Saint Helens One of the best-known volcanoes in the Ring of Fire is Mount Saint Helens in Washington State. Mount Saint Helens had been dormant, or quiet, since 1857. Then in March 1980, it began spitting out puffs of steam and ash. Officials warned people to leave the area. Scientists brought in equipment to measure the growing bulge in the mountainside. Everyone feared the volcano might erupt at any moment.

On May 18, after a sudden earthquake, Mount Saint Helens let loose a massive explosion of rock and lava. Heat from the blast melted snow on the mountain, which

Ring of Fire

map zone

- Plate boundary line
- Earthquakes
- Active volcanoes

Asia
North America
PACIFIC OCEAN
South America
Australia
Antarctica

THE WORLD ALMANAC Facts about the World — Major Eruptions in the Ring of Fire

Volcano	Year
Tambora, Indonesia	1815
Krakatau, Indonesia	1883
Mount Saint Helens, United States	**1980**
Nevado del Ruiz, Colombia	1985
Mount Pinatubo, Philippines	1991

hmhsocialstudies.com

Mount Saint Helens, 1980
The 1980 eruption of Mount Saint Helens blew ash and hot gases miles into the air. Today, scientists study the volcano to learn more about predicting eruptions.

mixed with ash to create deadly mudflows. As the mud quickly poured downhill, it flattened forests, swept away cars, and destroyed buildings. Clouds of ash covered the land, killing crops, clogging waterways, and blanketing towns as far as 200 miles (330 km) away. When the volcano finally quieted down, 57 people had died. Damage totaled nearly $1 billion. If it were not for the early evacuation of the area, the destruction could have been much worse.

What It Means By studying Mount Saint Helens, scientists learned a great deal about stratovolcanoes. These are tall, steep, cone-shaped volcanoes that have violent eruptions. Stratovolcanoes often form in areas where tectonic plates collide.

Because stratovolcanoes often produce deadly eruptions, scientists try to predict when they might erupt. The lessons learned from Mount Saint Helens helped scientists

warn people about another stratovolcano, Mount Pinatubo in the Philippines. That eruption in 1991 was the second-largest of the 1900s. It was far from the deadliest, however. Careful observation and timely warnings saved thousands of lives.

The Ring of Fire will always remain a threat. However, the better we understand its volcanoes, the better prepared we'll be when they erupt.

Geography for Life Activity

1. How did the eruption of Mount Saint Helens affect the surrounding area?

2. Why do scientists monitor volcanic activity?

3. **Investigating the Effects of Volcanoes** Some volcanic eruptions affect environmental conditions around the world. Research the eruption of either Mount Saint Helens or the Philippines' Mount Pinatubo to find out how its eruption affected the global environment.

Social Studies Skills

Using a Physical Map

Learn

Physical maps show important physical features, like oceans and mountains, in a particular area. They also indicate an area's elevation, or the height of the land in relation to sea level.

When you use a physical map, there are important pieces of information you should always examine.

- Identify physical features. Natural features, such as mountains, rivers, and lakes, are labeled on physical maps. Read the labels carefully to identify what physical features are present.

- Read the legend. On physical maps, the legend indicates scale as well as elevation. The different colors in the elevation key indicate how far above or below sea level a place is.

Practice

Use the physical map of India at right to answer the questions below.

1 What landforms and bodies of water are indicated on the map?

2 What is the highest elevation in India? Where is it located?

India: Physical

Kanchenjunga 28,208 ft (8,598 m)

ELEVATION
Feet		Meters
13,120		4,000
6,560		2,000
1,640		500
656		200
(Sea level) 0		0 (Sea level)

0 250 500 Miles
0 250 500 Kilometers

Projection: Lambert Conformal Conic

Apply

Locate the physical map of Africa in the atlas in the back of the book. Use the map to answer the questions below.

1. Which region has the highest elevation?

2. What bodies of water surround Africa?

3. What large island is located off the east coast of Africa?

Chapter Review

Geography's Impact
video series
Review the video to answer the closing question:
What are some reasons for water shortages, and what can be done to solve this problem?

Visual Summary

Use the visual summary below to help you review the main ideas of the chapter.

QUICK FACTS

The amount of solar energy Earth receives changes based on Earth's movement and position.

Water is crucial to life on Earth. Our abundant water supply is stored in oceans, in lakes, and underground.

Earth's various landforms are shaped by complex processes both under and on the planet's surface.

Reviewing Vocabulary, Terms, and Places

For each statement below, write T if it is true and F if it is false. If the statement is false, write the correct term that would make the sentence a true statement.

1. **Weathering** is the movement of sediment from one location to another.

2. Because high **latitude** areas receive indirect rays from the sun, they have cooler temperatures.

3. Most of our **groundwater** is stored in Earth's streams, rivers, and lakes.

4. It takes 365¼ days for Earth to complete one **rotation** around the sun.

5. Streams are formed when **precipitation** collects in narrow channels.

6. **Earthquakes** cause erosion as they flow downhill, carving valleys and mountain peaks.

7. The planet's tilt affects the amount of **erosion** Earth receives from the sun.

Comprehension and Critical Thinking

SECTION 1 *(Pages 26–29)*

8. **a. Identify** What factors influence the amount of energy that different places on Earth receive from the sun?

b. Analyze Why do the Northern and Southern hemispheres experience opposite seasons?

c. Predict What might happen to the amount of solar energy we receive if Earth's axis were straight up and down?

SECTION 2 *(Pages 30–34)*

9. **a. Describe** What different sources of water are available on Earth?

b. Draw Conclusions How does the water cycle keep Earth's water supply relatively constant?

c. Elaborate What water problems affect people around the world? What solutions can you think of for one of those problems?

SECTION 3 *(Pages 35–41)*

10. a. Define What is a landform? What are some common types of landforms?

b. Analyze Why are Earth's landforms still changing?

c. Elaborate What physical features dominate the landscape in your community? How do they affect life there?

Using the Internet 21ST CENTURY

11. Activity: Researching Earth's Seasons Earth's seasons not only affect temperatures, they also affect how much daylight is available during specific times of the year. Through your online textbook, research Earth's seasons and view animations to see how seasons change. Then use the interactive worksheet to answer some questions about what you learned.

↗ hmhsocialstudies.com

Social Studies Skills

Using a Physical Map *Examine the physical map of the United States in the back of this book. Use it to answer the questions below.*

12. What physical feature extends along the Gulf of Mexico?

13. What mountain range in the West lies above 6,560 feet?

14. Where does the elevation drop below sea level?

Map Activity 21ST CENTURY

Physical Map *Use the map on the right to answer the questions that follow.*

15. Which letter indicates a river?

16. Which letter on the map indicates the highest elevation?

17. The lowest elevation on the map is indicated by which letter?

18. An island is indicated by which letter?

19. Which letter indicates a large body of water?

20. Which letter indicates an area of land between 1,640 feet and 6,560 feet above sea level?

ELEVATION
Feet		Meters
13,120		4,000
6,560		2,000
1,640		500
656		200
(Sea level) 0		0 (Sea level)
Below sea level		Below sea level

0   250   500   750 Miles
0   250   500   750 Kilometers
Projection: Two-Point Equidistant

FOCUS ON READING AND WRITING

Using Word Parts *Use what you learned about prefixes, suffixes, and word roots to answer the questions below.*

21. The prefix *in-* means not. What do the words *invisible* and *inactive* mean?

22. The suffix *-ment* means action or process. What does the word *movement* mean?"

23. Writing a Haiku Look back through your notes about Earth. Choose one aspect of Earth to describe in a haiku. A haiku is a three-line poem that consists of 17 syllables—five in the first line, seven in the second line, and five in the third line. Be sure to use descriptive words to paint a picture of planet Earth.

Standardized Test Prep

DIRECTIONS: Read questions 1 through 7 and write the letter of the best response. Then read question 8 and write your own well-constructed response.

1 **Which regions on Earth have seasons tied to the amount of rainfall?**

A polar regions

B the tropics

C the Northern Hemisphere

D high latitudes

2 **Most of Earth's water supply is made up of**

A groundwater.

B water vapor.

C freshwater.

D salt water.

3 **The theory of continental drift explains how**

A Earth's continents have moved thousands of miles.

B Earth's axis has moved to its current position.

C mountains and valleys are formed.

D sediment moves from one place to another.

4 **Which of the following is a cause of erosion?**

A evaporation

B ice

C plate collisions

D Earth's tilt

5 **Changes in solar energy that create day and night are a result of**

A the movement of tectonic plates.

B Earth's rotation.

C the revolution of Earth around the sun.

D Earth's tilt.

The Water Cycle

6 **In the illustration above, which letter *best* reflects the process of evaporation?**

A W

B X

C Y

D Z

7 **Which of the following is *most likely* a cause of water pollution?**

A River water is used to produce electricity.

B Heavy rainfall causes a river to overflow its banks.

C Chemicals from a factory seep into the local water supply.

D Groundwater is used faster than it can be replaced.

8 **Extended Response Question** Use the water cycle diagram above to explain how Earth's water cycle affects our water supply.

Climate, Environment, and Resources

Essential Question What factors shape Earth's different environments?

 ## What You Will Learn...

In this chapter you will learn about weather and climate. You will also learn about how living things and the environment are connected and about natural resources.

FOCUS ON READING AND VIEWING

Understanding Cause and Effect A cause makes something happen. An effect is the result of a cause. Words such as *because*, *result*, *since*, and *therefore* can signal causes or effects. As you read, look for causes and effects to understand how things relate. **See the lesson, Understanding Cause and Effect, on page 108.**

Writing a Weather Report You have likely seen a TV weather report, which tells the current weather conditions and predicts future conditions. After reading this chapter, prepare a weather report for a reason and place of your choosing. Present your report to the class and then view your classmates' reports.

Climate Earth has many climates, such as the dry climate of the region shown here.

HISTORY. **Tornado Alley Twister**

⬈ hmhsocialstudies.com VIDEO

ANALYSIS
SKILL **ANALYZING VISUALS**

This photo shows a severe thunderstorm. These storms produce violent weather, such as heavy rainfall and strong winds, which affects people's lives.

How do you think this storm might have affected the people who lived in this area?

Environments Living things, such as this koala, depend on their surroundings.

Natural Resources Earth provides many valuable and useful natural resources, such as oil.

Weather and Climate

What You Will Learn...

Main Ideas

1. While weather is short term, climate is a region's average weather over a long period.
2. The amount of sun at a given location is affected by Earth's tilt, movement, and shape.
3. Wind and water move heat around Earth, affecting how warm or wet a place is.
4. Mountains influence temperature and precipitation.

The Big Idea

The sun, location, wind, water, and mountains affect weather and climate.

Key Terms

weather, *p. 50*
climate, *p. 50*
prevailing winds, *p. 51*
ocean currents, *p. 52*
front, *p. 53*

hmhsocialstudies.com
TAKING NOTES

Use the graphic organizer online to take notes on the factors that affect weather and climate.

If **YOU** lived there...

You live in Buffalo, New York, at the eastern end of Lake Erie. One evening in January, you are watching the local TV news. The weather forecaster says, "A huge storm is brewing in the Midwest and moving east. As usual, winds from this storm will drop several feet of snow on Buffalo as they blow off Lake Erie."

Why will winds off the lake drop snow on Buffalo?

BUILDING BACKGROUND All life on Earth depends on the sun's energy and on the cycle of water from the land to the air and back again. In addition, sun and water work with other forces, such as wind, to create global patterns of weather and climate.

Understanding Weather and Climate

"Climate is what you expect; weather is what you get."
—Robert Heinlein, from *Time Enough for Love*

What is it like outside right now where you live? Is it hot, sunny, wet, cold? Is this what it is usually like outside for this time of year? The first two questions are about **weather**, the short-term changes in the air for a given place and time. The last question is about **climate**, a region's average weather conditions over a long period.

Weather is the temperature and precipitation from hour to hour or day to day. "Today is sunny, but tomorrow it might rain" is a statement about weather. Climate is the expected weather for a place based on data and experience. "Summer here is usually hot and muggy" is a statement about climate. The factors that shape weather and climate include the sun, location on Earth, wind, water, and mountains.

READING CHECK **Finding Main Ideas** How are weather and climate different from each other?

Sun and Location

Energy from the sun heats the planet. Different locations receive different amounts of sunlight, though. Thus, some locations are warmer than others. The differences are due to Earth's tilt, movement, and shape.

You have learned that Earth is tilted on its axis. The part of Earth tilted toward the sun receives more solar energy than the part tilted away from the sun. As the Earth revolves around the sun, the part of Earth that is tilted toward the sun changes during the year. This process creates the seasons. In general, temperatures in summer are warmer than in winter.

Earth's shape also affects the amount of sunlight different locations receive. Because Earth is a sphere, its surface is rounded. Therefore, solar rays are more direct and concentrated near the equator. Nearer the poles, the sun's rays are less direct and more spread out.

As a result, areas near the equator, called the lower latitudes, are mainly hot year-round. Areas near the poles, called the higher latitudes, are cold year-round. Areas about halfway between the equator and poles have more seasonal change. In general, the farther from the equator, or the higher the latitude, the colder the climate.

READING CHECK **Summarizing** How does Earth's tilt on its axis affect climate?

Wind and Water

Heat from the sun moves across Earth's surface. The reason is that air and water warmed by the sun are constantly on the move. You might have seen a gust of wind or a stream of water carrying dust or dirt. In a similar way, wind and water carry heat from place to place. As a result, they make different areas of Earth warmer or cooler.

Global Wind Systems

Prevailing winds blow in circular belts across Earth. These belts occur at about every 30° of latitude.

ANALYZING VISUALS Which direction do the prevailing winds blow across the United States?

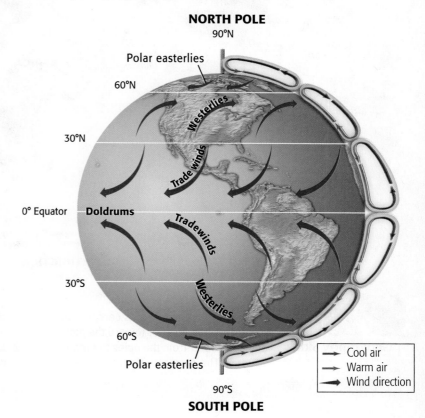

NORTH POLE
90°N
Polar easterlies
60°N
Westerlies
30°N
Trade winds
0° Equator   Doldrums
Tradewinds
30°S
Westerlies
60°S
Polar easterlies
90°S
SOUTH POLE

→ Cool air
→ Warm air
→ Wind direction

Global Winds

Wind, or the sideways movement of air, blows in great streams around the planet. **Prevailing winds** are winds that blow in the same direction over large areas of Earth. The diagram above shows the patterns of Earth's prevailing winds.

To understand Earth's wind patterns, you need to think about the weight of air. Although you cannot feel it, air has weight. This weight changes with the temperature. Cold air is heavier than warm air. For this reason, when air cools, it gets heavier and sinks. When air warms, it gets lighter and rises. As warm air rises, cooler air moves in to take its place, creating wind.

Warm current
Cold current

Arctic Ocean

NORTH AMERICA

EUROPE

ASIA

North Pacific Ocean

North Atlantic Ocean

AFRICA

Equator

SOUTH AMERICA

South Pacific Ocean

South Atlantic Ocean

AUSTRALIA

Southern Ocean

ANTARCTICA

map zone
Geography Skills

Movement Ocean currents carry warm water from the equator toward the poles and cold water from the poles toward the equator. The currents affect temperature.

1. **Use the Map** Does a warm or cold ocean current flow along the lower west coast of North America?
2. **Explain** How do ocean currents move heat between warmer and colder areas of Earth?

FOCUS ON READING

What is the effect of Earth's rotation on prevailing winds?

On a global scale, this rising, sinking, and flowing of air creates Earth's prevailing wind patterns. At the equator, hot air rises and flows toward the poles. At the poles, cold air sinks and flows toward the equator. Meanwhile, Earth is rotating. Earth's rotation causes prevailing winds to curve east or west rather than flowing directly north or south.

Depending on their source, prevailing winds make a region warmer or colder. In addition, the source of the winds can make a region drier or wetter. Winds that form from warm air or pass over lots of water often carry moisture. In contrast, winds that form from cold air or pass over lots of land often are dry.

Ocean Currents

Like wind, **ocean currents**—large streams of surface seawater—move heat around Earth. Winds drive these currents. The map above shows how Earth's ocean currents carry warm or cool water to different areas. The water's temperature affects air temperature near it. Warm currents raise temperatures; cold currents lower them.

The Gulf Stream is a warm current that flows north along the U.S. East Coast. It then flows east across the Atlantic to become the North Atlantic Drift. As the warm current flows along northwestern Europe, it heats the air. Westerlies blow the warmed air across Europe. This process makes Europe warmer than it otherwise would be.

Large Bodies of Water

Large bodies of water, such as an ocean or sea, also affect climate. Water heats and cools more slowly than land does. For this reason, large bodies of water make the temperature of the land nearby milder. Thus, coastal areas, such as the California coast, usually do not have as wide temperature ranges as inland areas.

As an example, the state of Michigan is largely surrounded by the Great Lakes. The lakes make temperatures in the state milder than other places as far north.

Wind, Water, and Storms

If you watch weather reports, you will hear about storms moving across the United States. Tracking storms is important to us because the United States has so many of them. As you will see, some areas of the world have more storms than others do.

Most storms occur when two air masses collide. An air mass is a large body of air. The place where two air masses of different temperatures or moisture content meet is a **front**. Cold air masses from the North and warm air masses from the South frequently collide over the United States, producing dramatic storms.

Fronts can produce rain or snow as well as severe weather such as thunderstorms and icy blizzards. Thunderstorms produce rain, lightning, and thunder. In the United States, they are most common in spring and summer. Blizzards produce strong winds and large amounts of snow and are most common during winter.

Thunderstorms and blizzards can also produce tornadoes, another type of severe storm. A tornado is a small, rapidly twisting funnel of air that touches the ground. Tornadoes usually affect a limited area and last only a few minutes. However, they can be highly destructive, uprooting trees and tossing large vehicles through the air.

Tornadoes can be extremely deadly as well. In 1925 a tornado that crossed Missouri, Illinois, and Indiana left 695 people dead. It is the deadliest U.S. tornado on record.

The largest and most destructive storms, however, are hurricanes. These large, rotating storms form over tropical waters in the Atlantic Ocean, usually from late summer to fall. Did you know that hurricanes and typhoons are the same? Typhoons are just hurricanes that form in the Pacific Ocean.

Extreme Weather

Severe weather is often dangerous and destructive. In the top photo, rescuers search for people during a flood in Yardley, Pennsylvania. Below, a tornado races across a wheat field.

53

Rain Shadow Effect

Snow

Warming dry air

Rain

Cooling moist air

Rain Shadow

Most of the moisture in the ocean air falls on the mountainside facing the wind. LIttle moisture remains to fall on the other side, creating a rain shadow.

Hurricanes produce drenching rain and strong winds that can reach speeds of 155 miles per hour (250 kph) or more. This is more than twice as fast as most people drive on highways. In addition, hurricanes form tall walls of water called storm surges. When a storm surge smashes into land, it can wipe out an entire coastal area.

READING CHECK **Analyzing** Why do coastal areas have milder climates than inland areas?

Mountains

Mountains can influence an area's climate by affecting both temperature and precipitation. Many high mountains are located in warm areas yet have snow at the top all year. How can this be? The reason is that temperature decreases with elevation—the height on Earth's surface above sea level.

Mountains also create wet and dry areas. Look at the diagram at left. A mountain forces air blowing against it to rise. As it rises, the air cools and precipitation falls as rain or snow. Thus, the side of the mountain facing the wind is often green and lush. However, little moisture remains for the other side. This effect creates a rain shadow, a dry area on the mountainside facing away from the direction of the wind.

READING CHECK **Finding Main Ideas** How does temperature change with elevation?

SUMMARY AND PREVIEW As you can see, the sun, location on Earth, wind, water, and mountains affect weather and climate. In the next section you will learn what the world's different climate regions are like.

Section 1 Assessment

Reviewing Ideas, Terms, and Places

1. **a. Recall** What shapes **weather** and **climate**?
   b. Contrast How do weather and climate differ?
2. **a. Identify** What parts of Earth receive the most heat from the sun?
   b. Explain Why do the poles receive less solar energy than the equator does?
3. **a. Describe** What creates wind?
   b. Summarize How do **ocean currents** and large bodies of water affect climate?
4. **a. Define** What is a rain shadow?
   b. Explain Why might a mountaintop and a nearby valley have widely different temperatures?

Critical Thinking

5. **Identifying Cause and Effect** Draw a chart like this one. Use your notes to explain how each factor affects climate.

	Effect on Climate
Sun and Location	
Wind	
Water	
Mountains	

FOCUS ON VIEWING

6. **Writing about Weather and Climate** Jot down information to include in your weather report. For example, you might want to include a term such as fronts or describe certain types of storms such as hurricanes or tornadoes.

World Climates

If YOU lived there...

You live in Colorado and are on your first serious hike in the Rocky Mountains. Since it is July, it is hot in the campground in the valley. But your guide insists that you bring a heavy fleece jacket. By noon, you have climbed to 11,000 feet. You are surprised to see patches of snow in shady spots. Suddenly, you are very happy that you brought your jacket!

Why does it get colder as you climb higher?

BUILDING BACKGROUND While weather is the day-to-day changes in a certain area, climate is the average weather conditions over a long period. Earth's different climates depend partly on the amount of sunlight a region receives. Differences in climate also depend on factors such as wind, water, and elevation.

Major Climate Zones

In January, how will you dress for the weekend? In some places, you might get dressed to go skiing. In other places, you might head out in a swimsuit to go to the beach. What the seasons are like where you live depends on climate.

Earth is a patchwork of climates. Geographers identify these climates by looking at temperature, precipitation, and native plant life. Using these items, we can divide Earth into five general climate zones—tropical, temperate, polar, dry, and highland.

The first three climate zones relate to latitude. Tropical climates occur near the equator, in the low latitudes. Temperate climates occur about halfway between the equator and the poles, in the middle latitudes. Polar climates occur near the poles, in the high latitudes. The last two climate zones occur at many different latitudes. In addition, geographers divide some climate zones into more specific climate regions. The chart and map on the next two pages describe the world's climate regions.

READING CHECK Drawing Inferences Why do you think geographers consider native plant life when categorizing climates?

What You Will Learn...

Main Ideas

1. Geographers use temperature, precipitation, and plant life to identify climate zones.
2. Tropical climates are wet and warm, while dry climates receive little or no rain.
3. Temperate climates have the most seasonal change.
4. Polar climates are cold and dry, while highland climates change with elevation.

The Big Idea

Earth's five major climate zones are identified by temperature, precipitation, and plant life.

Key Terms

monsoons, *p. 58*
savannas, *p. 58*
steppes, *p. 59*
permafrost, *p. 61*

hmhsocialstudies.com
TAKING NOTES

Use the graphic organizer online to take notes on Earth's major climate zones.

World Climate Regions

To explore the world's climate regions, start with the chart below. After reading about each climate region, locate the places on the map that have that climate. As you locate climates, look for patterns. For example, places near the equator tend to have warmer climates than places near the poles. See if you can identify some other climate patterns.

Tropical climate

	Climate	Where is it?	What is it like?	Plants
Tropical	HUMID TROPICAL	On and near the equator	Warm with high amounts of rain year-round; in a few places, monsoons create extreme wet seasons	Tropical rain forest
	TROPICAL SAVANNA	Higher latitudes in the tropics	Warm all year; distinct rainy and dry seasons; at least 20 inches (50 cm) of rain during the summer	Tall grasses and scattered trees
Dry	DESERT	Mainly center on 30° latitude; also in middle of continents, on west coasts, or in rain shadows	Sunny and dry; less than 10 inches (25 cm) of rain a year; hot in the tropics; cooler with wide daytime temperature ranges in middle latitudes	A few hardy plants, such as cacti
	STEPPE	Mainly bordering deserts and interiors of large continents	About 10–20 inches (25–50 cm) of precipitation a year; hot summers and cooler winters with wide temperature ranges during the day	Shorter grasses; some trees and shrubs by water
Temperate	MEDITERRANEAN	West coasts in middle latitudes	Dry, sunny, warm summers; mild, wetter winters; rain averages 15–20 inches (30–50 cm) a year	Scrub woodland and grassland
	HUMID SUBTROPICAL	East coasts in middle latitudes	Humid with hot summers and mild winters; rain year-round; in paths of hurricanes and typhoons	Mixed forest
	MARINE WEST COAST	West coasts in the upper-middle latitudes	Cloudy, mild summers and cool, rainy winters; strong ocean influence	Evergreen forests
	HUMID CONTINENTAL	East coasts and interiors of upper-middle latitudes	Four distinct seasons; long, cold winters and short, warm summers; average precipitation varies	Mixed forest

Polar climate

Dry climate

Climate		Where is it?	What is it like?	Plants
Polar	SUBARCTIC	Higher latitudes of the interior and east coasts of continents	Extremes of temperature; long, cold winters and short, warm summers; little precipitation	Northern ever-green forests
	TUNDRA	Coasts in high latitudes	Cold all year; very long, cold winters and very short, cool summers; little precipitation; permafrost	Moss, lichens, low shrubs
	ICE CAP	Polar regions	Freezing cold; snow and ice; little precipitation	No vegetation
Highland	HIGHLAND	High mountain regions	Wide range of temperatures and precipitation amounts, depending on elevation and location	Ranges from forest to tundra

Geography Skills

Regions Note how Earth's climate regions relate to different locations.

1. **Locate** Which climates are found mainly in the Northern Hemisphere?

2. **Identify** What climate does most of northern Africa have?

3. **Make Generalizations** Where are many of the world's driest climates found on Earth?

4. **Interpreting Charts** Examine the chart. Which two climates have the least amount of vegetation?

↗ hmhsocialstudies.com

The Tuareg of the Sahara.

In the Sahara, the world's largest desert, temperatures can top 130°F (54°C). Yet the Tuareg (TWAH-reg) of North and West Africa call the Sahara home—and prefer it. The Tuareg have raised camels and other animals in the Sahara for more than 1,000 years. The animals graze on sparse desert plants. When the plants are gone, the Tuareg move on.

In camp, Tuareg families live in tents made from animal skins. Some wealthier Tuareg live in adobe homes. The men traditionally wear blue veils wrapped around their face and head. The veils help protect against windblown desert dust.

Summarizing How have the Tuareg adapted to life in a desert?

Tropical and Dry Climates

Are you the type of person who likes to go to extremes? Then tropical and dry climates might be for you. These climates include the wettest, driest, and hottest places on Earth.

Tropical Climates

Our tour of Earth's climates starts at the equator, in the heart of the tropics. This region extends from the Tropic of Cancer to the Tropic of Capricorn. Look back at the map to locate this region.

Humid Tropical Climate At the equator, the hot, damp air hangs like a thick, wet blanket. Sweat quickly coats your body.

Welcome to the humid tropical climate. This climate is warm, muggy, and rainy year-round. Temperatures average about 80°F (26°C). Showers or storms occur almost daily, and rainfall ranges from 70 to more than 450 inches (180 to 1,140 cm) a year. In comparison, only a few parts of the United States average more than 70 inches (180 cm) of rain a year.

Some places with a humid tropical climate have **monsoons**, seasonal winds that bring either dry or moist air. During one part of the year, a moist ocean wind creates an extreme wet season. The winds then shift direction, and a dry land wind creates a dry season. Monsoons affect several parts of Asia. For example, the town of Mawsynram, India, receives on average more than 450 inches (1,140 cm) of rain a year—all in about six months! That is about 37 feet (11 m) of rain. As you can imagine, flooding during wet seasons is common and can be severe.

The humid tropical climate's warm temperatures and heavy rainfall support tropical rain forests. These lush forests contain more types of plants and animals than anywhere else on Earth. The world's largest rain forest is in the Amazon River basin in South America. There you can find more than 50,000 species, including giant lily pads, poisonous tree frogs, and toucans.

Tropical Savanna Climate Moving north and south away from the equator, we find the tropical savanna climate. This climate has a long, hot, dry season followed by short periods of rain. Rainfall is much lower than at the equator but still high. Temperatures are hot in the summer, often as high as 90°F (32°C). Winters are cooler but rarely get cold.

This climate does not receive enough rainfall to support dense forests. Instead, it supports **savannas**—areas of tall grasses and scattered trees and shrubs.

Dry Climates

Leaving Earth's wettest places, we head to its driest. These climates are found in a number of locations on the planet.

Desert Climate Picture the sun baking down on a barren wasteland. This is the desert, Earth's hottest and driest climate. Deserts receive less than 10 inches (25 cm) of rain a year. Dry air and clear skies produce high daytime temperatures and rapid cooling at night. In some deserts, highs can top 130°F (54°C)! Under such conditions, only very hardy plants and animals can live. Many plants grow far apart so as not to compete for water. Others, such as cacti, store water in fleshy stems and leaves.

Steppe Climate Semidry grasslands or prairies—called **steppes** (STEPS)—often border deserts. Steppes receive slightly more rain than deserts do. Short grasses are the most common plants, but shrubs and trees grow along streams and rivers.

> **READING CHECK** **Contrasting** What are some ways in which tropical and dry climates differ?

Temperate Climates

If you enjoy hot, sunny days as much as chilly, rainy ones, then temperate climates are for you. *Temperate* means "moderate" or "mild." These mild climates tend to have four seasons, with warm or hot summers and cool or cold winters.

Temperate climates occur in the middle latitudes, the regions halfway between the equator and the poles. Air masses from the tropics and the poles often meet in these regions, which creates a number of different temperate climates. You very likely live in one, because most Americans do.

Mediterranean Climate Named for the region of the Mediterranean Sea, this sunny, pleasant climate is found in many popular vacation areas. In a Mediterranean climate, summers are hot, dry, and sunny. Winters are mild and somewhat wet. Plant life includes shrubs and short trees with scattered larger trees. The Mediterranean climate occurs mainly in coastal areas. In the United States, much of California has this climate.

Mediterranean Climate

The climate graph shows average temperatures and precipitation for Nice (NEECE), France, which has a Mediterranean climate.

ANALYZING GRAPHS During which month is precipitation lowest?

Climate Graph for Nice, France

Source: The Weather Channel Interactive, Inc.

Highland Climates

Mount Kilimanjaro is the tallest mountain in Africa. Although Kilimanjaro is only about 200 miles (320 km) south of the equator, snow blankets its highest peak.

Kilimanjaro rises to 19,341 ft (5,895 m). The snow-covered summit has an ice cap climate.

Climate and plant life ranges from rain forest, to steppe, to desert, to tundra.

A tropical savanna climate is found around the base of Mount Kilimanjaro.

ANALYSIS SKILL **ANALYZING VISUALS**

Which type of climate is found on the top of Mount Kilimanjaro?

Humid Subtropical Climate The southeastern United States is an example of the humid subtropical climate. This climate occurs along east coasts near the tropics. In these areas, warm, moist air blows in from the ocean. Summers are hot and muggy. Winters are mild, with occasional frost and snow. Storms occur year-round. In addition, hurricanes can strike, bringing violent winds, heavy rain, and high seas.

A humid subtropical climate supports mixed forests. These forests include both deciduous trees, which lose their leaves each fall, and coniferous trees, which are green year-round. Coniferous trees are also known as evergreens.

Marine West Coast Climate Parts of North America's Pacific coast and of western Europe have a marine west coast climate. This climate occurs on west coasts where winds carry moisture in from the seas.

The moist air keeps temperatures mild year-round. Winters are foggy, cloudy, and rainy, while summers can be warm and sunny. Dense evergreen forests thrive in this climate.

Humid Continental Climate Closer to the poles, in the upper-middle latitudes, many inland and east coast areas have a humid continental climate. This climate has four **distinct** seasons. Summers are short and hot. Spring and fall are mild, and winters are long, cold, and in general, snowy.

This climate's rainfall supports vast grasslands and forests. Grasses can grow very tall, such as in parts of the American Great Plains. Forests contain both deciduous and coniferous trees, with coniferous forests occurring in the colder areas.

ACADEMIC VOCABULARY

distinct clearly different and separate

READING CHECK **Categorizing** Which of the temperate climates is too dry to support forests?

Polar and Highland Climates

Get ready to feel the chill as we end our tour in the polar and highland climates. The three polar climates are found in the high latitudes near the poles. The varied highland climate is found on mountains.

Subarctic Climate The subarctic climate and the tundra climate described below occur mainly in the Northern Hemisphere south of the Arctic Ocean. In the subarctic climate, winters are long and bitterly cold. Summers are short and cool. Temperatures stay below freezing for about half the year. The climate's moderate rainfall supports vast evergreen forests, or taiga (TY-guh).

Tundra Climate The tundra climate occurs in coastal areas along the Arctic Ocean. As in the subarctic climate, winters are long and bitterly cold. Temperatures rise above freezing only during the short summer. Rainfall is light, and only plants such as mosses, lichens, and small shrubs grow.

In parts of the tundra, soil layers stay frozen all year. Permanently frozen layers of soil are called **permafrost**. Frozen earth absorbs water poorly, which creates ponds and marshes in summer. This moisture causes plants to burst forth in bloom.

Ice Cap Climate The harshest places on Earth may be the North and South poles. These regions have an ice cap climate. Temperatures are bone-numbingly cold, and lows of more than –120°F (–84°C) have been recorded. Snow and ice remain year-round, but precipitation is light. Not surprisingly, no vegetation grows. However, mammals such as penguins and polar bears thrive.

Highland Climates The highland climate includes polar climates plus others. In fact, this mountain climate is actually several climates in one. As you go up a mountain, the climate changes. Temperatures drop, and plant life grows sparser. Going up a mountain can be like going from the tropics to the poles. On very tall mountains, ice coats the summit year-round.

FOCUS ON READING
What is the effect of elevation on climate?

READING CHECK **Comparing** How are polar and highland climates similar?

SUMMARY AND PREVIEW As you can see, Earth has many climates, which we identify based on temperature, precipitation, and native plant life. In the next section you will read about how nature and all living things are connected.

Section 2 Assessment

hmhsocialstudies.com
ONLINE QUIZ

Reviewing Ideas, Terms, and Places

1. a. Recall Which three major climate zones occur at certain latitudes?
b. Summarize How do geographers categorize Earth's different climates?
2. a. Define What are **monsoons**?
b. Make Inferences In which type of dry climate do you think the fewest people live, and why?
3. a. Identify What are the four temperate climates?
b. Draw Conclusions Why are places with a Mediterranean climate popular vacation spots?
4. a. Describe What are some effects of **permafrost**?
b. Explain How are highland climates unique?

Critical Thinking

5. Categorizing Create a chart like the one below for each climate region. Then use your notes to describe each climate region's average temperatures, precipitation, and native plant life.

Climate Region →	Temperature	Precipitation	Plant Life

FOCUS ON VIEWING

6. Discussing World Climates Add information about the climate of the place you have selected, such as average temperature and precipitation.

Natural Environments

What You Will Learn...

Main Ideas

1. The environment and life are interconnected and exist in a fragile balance.
2. Soils play an important role in the environment.

The Big Idea

Plants, animals, and the environment, including soil, interact and affect one another.

Key Terms

environment, *p. 62*
ecosystem, *p. 63*
habitat, *p. 64*
extinct, *p. 64*
humus, *p. 65*
desertification, *p. 65*

hmhsocialstudies.com
TAKING NOTES

Use the graphic organizer online to take notes on Earth's natural environments.

If YOU lived there...

When your family moved to the city, you were sure you would miss the woods and pond near your old house. Then one of your new friends at school told you there's a large park only a few blocks away. You wondered how interesting a city park could be. But you were surprised at the many plants and animals that live there.

What environments might you see in the park?

BUILDING BACKGROUND No matter where you live, you are part of a natural environment. From a desert to a rain forest to a city park, every environment is home to a unique community of plant and animal life. These plants and animals live in balance with nature.

The Environment and Life

If you saw a wild polar bear outside your school, you would likely be shocked. In most parts of the United States, polar bears live only in zoos. This is because plants and animals must live where they are suited to the **environment**, or surroundings. Polar bears are suited to very cold places with lots of ice, water, and fish. As you will see, living things and their environments are connected and affect each other in many ways.

Limits on Life

The environment limits life. As our tour of the world's climates showed, factors such as temperature, rainfall, and soil conditions limit where plants and animals can live. Palm trees cannot survive at the frigid North Pole. Ferns will quickly wilt and die in deserts, but they thrive in tropical rain forests.

At the same time, all plants and animals are adapted to specific environments. For example, kangaroo rats are adapted to dry desert environments. These small rodents can get all the water they need from food, so they seldom have to drink water.

Connections in Nature

The interconnections between living things and the environment form ecosystems. An **ecosystem** is a group of plants and animals that depend on each other for survival and the environment in which they live. Ecosystems can be any size and can occur wherever air, water, and soil support life. A garden pond, a city park, a prairie, and a rain forest are all examples of ecosystems.

The diagram below shows a forest ecosystem. Each part of this ecosystem fills a certain role. The sun provides energy to the plants, which use the energy to make their own food. The plants then serve as food, either directly or indirectly, for all other life in the forest. When the plants and animals die, their remains break down and provide nutrients for the soil and new plant growth. Thus, the cycle continues.

Close-up

A Forest Ecosystem

A forest is one type of ecosystem. The plants and animals in the forest depend on one another and the forest environment for survival.

1 Sunlight is the source of energy for most living things.

2 Plants use the energy in sunlight to make food. They serve as the basis for other life in the ecosystem.

3 Animals such as rabbits eat plants and gain some of their energy.

4 Predators, such as wolves and hawks, eat rabbits and other prey for energy.

5 Larger predators, such as mountain lions, compete for the prey that is available.

ANALYSIS SKILL **ANALYZING VISUALS**

What might happen in the forest ecosystem above if the number of rabbits fell significantly?

Changes to Environments

The interconnected parts of an ecosystem exist in a fragile balance. For this reason, a small change to one part can affect the whole system. A lack of rain in the forest ecosystem could kill off many of the plants that feed the rabbits. If the rabbits die, there will be less food for the wolves and mountain lions. Then they too may die.

Many actions can affect ecosystems. For example, people need places to live and food to eat, so they clear land for homes and farms. Clearing land has **consequences**, however. It can cause the soil to erode. In addition, the plants and animals that live in the area might be left without food and shelter.

Actions such as clearing land and polluting can destroy habitats. A **habitat** is the place where a plant or animal lives. The most diverse habitats on Earth are tropical rain forests. People are clearing Earth's rain forests for farmland, lumber, and other reasons, though. As a result, these diverse habitats are being lost.

ACADEMIC VOCABULARY

consequences the effects of a particular event or events

FOCUS ON READING

What are some causes of habitat destruction?

Extreme changes in ecosystems can cause species to die out, or become **extinct**. As an example, flightless birds called dodos once lived on Mauritius (maw-RI-shuhs), an island in the Indian Ocean. When people began settling on the island, their actions harmed the dodos' habitat. First seen in 1507, dodos were extinct by 1681.

Recognizing these problems, many countries are working to balance people's needs with the needs of the environment. The United States, for example, has passed many laws to limit pollution, manage forests, and protect valuable ecosystems.

READING CHECK Drawing Inferences How might one change affect an entire ecosystem?

Soil and the Environment

As you know, plants are the basis for all food that animals eat. Soils help determine what plants will grow and how well. Because soils support plant life, they play an important role in the environment.

CONNECTING TO Science

Soil Factory

The next time you see a fallen tree in the forest, do not think of it as a dead log. Think of it as a soil factory. A fallen tree is buzzing with the activity of countless insects, bacteria, and other organisms. These organisms invade the fallen log and start to break the wood down.

As the tree decays and crumbles, it turns into humus. Humus is a rich blend of organic material. The humus mixes with the soil and broken rock material. These added nutrients then enrich the soil, making it possible for new trees and plants to grow. Fallen trees provide as much as one-third of the organic material in forest soil.

Summarizing What causes a fallen tree to change into soil?

Fertile soils are rich in minerals and **humus** (HYOO-muhs), decayed plant or animal matter. These soils can support abundant plant life. Like air and water, fertile soil is essential for life. Without it, we could not grow much of the food we eat.

Soils can lose fertility in several ways. Erosion from wind or water can sweep topsoil away. Planting the same crops over and over can also rob soil of its fertility. When soil becomes worn out, it cannot support as many plants. In fragile dry environments this can lead to the spread of desertlike conditions, or **desertification**. The spread of desertlike conditions is a serious problem in many parts of the world.

> **READING CHECK** **Analyzing** What do fertile soils contain, and why are these soils important?

SUMMARY AND PREVIEW Living things and the environment are connected, but changes can easily upset the balance in an ecosystem. Because they support plant life, soils are important parts of ecosystems. In the next section you will learn about Earth's many resources.

Soil Layers

The three layers of soil are the topsoil, subsoil, and broken rock. The thickness of each layer depends on the conditions in a specific location.

ANALYZING VISUALS In which layer of soil are most plant roots and insects found?

Topsoil

Subsoil

Broken Rock

Solid Rock

Section 3 Assessment

hmhsocialstudies.com
ONLINE QUIZ

Reviewing Ideas, Terms, and Places

1. **a. Define** What is an **ecosystem**, and what are two examples of ecosystems?
   b. Summarize How do nature and people change ecosystems?
   c. Elaborate Why can plants and animals not live everywhere?

2. **a. Recall** What is **humus**, and why is it important to soil?
   b. Identify Cause and Effect What actions can cause **desertification**, and what might be some possible effects?
   c. Elaborate Why is it important for geographers and scientists to study soils?

Critical Thinking

3. **Identifying Cause and Effect** Review your notes. Then use a chart like this one to identify some of the causes and effects of changes to ecosystems.

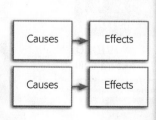

| Causes | → | Effects |

| Causes | → | Effects |

FOCUS ON VIEWING

4. **Writing about Natural Environments** Jot down ideas about how different types of weather might affect the environment of the place you chose. For example, how might lack of rain affect the area?

Earth's Changing Environments

PANGAEA

Pangaea About 250 million years ago, all of Earth's continents were connected, forming one giant landmass called Pangaea.

What was North America like 74 million years ago, when dinosaurs roamed Earth? You might be surprised to learn that it was a very different place. Earth's environments are always changing. The map at right shows North America in the age of dinosaurs. Back then, the climate was warm and humid, and large inland seas covered much of the land. The region's plants and animals were completely different. Slowly, however, things changed. Some major event, possibly an asteroid impact, wiped out the dinosaurs. Over time, North America's environments changed into the ones that exist today.

What Survived Dinosaurs, such as the plant-eating ceratopsian at left, are long gone. But insects, such as cockroaches and dragonflies, are still around.

G R E E N L A N D

Labrador Seaway

N O R T H

A M E R I C A

Western Interior Seaway

Hudson Seaway

COAST MOUNTAINS

SIERRA MADRE OCCIDENTAL

ROCKY MOUNTAINS

APPALACHIAN MOUNTAINS

North America in the Dinosaur Age Over time, Earth's continents slowly moved apart. About 74 million years ago, North America looked like the map at left. Inland seas covered parts of the continent. The map below shows North America today.

NORTH AMERICA TODAY

ANALYSIS SKILL **ANALYZING VISUALS**

1. **Name** What mountain ranges covered parts of North America 74 million years ago?
2. **Contrast** Based on the maps above, how has North America changed since the dinosaur age?

Natural Resources

If YOU lived there...

You live in Southern California, where the climate is warm and dry. Every week, you water the grass around your house to keep it green. Now the city has declared a "drought emergency" because of a lack of rain. City officials have put limits on watering lawns and on other uses of water.

How can you help conserve scarce water?

Earth's Valuable Resources

Think about the materials in nature that you use. You have learned about the many ways we use sun, water, and land. They are just a start, though. Look at the human-made products around you. They all required the use of natural materials in some way. We use trees to make paper for books. We use petroleum, or oil, to make plastics for cell phones. We use metals to make machines, which we then use to make many items. Without these materials, our lives would change drastically.

Using Natural Resources

Trees, oil, and metals are all examples of natural resources. A **natural resource** is any material in nature that people use and value. Earth's most important natural resources include air, water, soils, forests, and minerals.

Understanding how and why people use natural resources is an important part of geography. We use some natural resources just as they are, such as wind. Usually, though, we change natural resources to make something new. For example, we change metals to make products such as bicycles and watches. Thus, most natural resources are raw materials for other products.

What You Will Learn...

Main Ideas

1. Earth provides valuable resources for our use.
2. Energy resources provide fuel, heat, and electricity.
3. Mineral resources include metals, rocks, and salt.
4. Resources shape people's lives and countries' wealth.

The Big Idea

Earth's natural resources have many valuable uses, and their availability affects people in many ways.

Key Terms

natural resource, *p. 68*
renewable resources, *p. 69*
nonrenewable resources, *p. 69*
deforestation, *p. 69*
reforestation, *p. 69*
fossil fuels, *p. 69*
hydroelectric power, *p. 70*

hmhsocialstudies.com
TAKING NOTES

Use the graphic organizer online to take notes on Earth's resources.

Reforestation

Members of the Green Belt Movement plant trees in Kenya. Although trees are a renewable resource, some forests are being cut down faster than new trees can replace them. Reforestation helps protect Earth's valuable forestlands.

ANALYZING VISUALS How does reforestation help the environment?

Types of Natural Resources

We group natural resources into two types, those we can replace and those we cannot. **Renewable resources** are resources Earth replaces naturally. For example, when we cut down a tree, another tree can grow in its place. Renewable resources include water, soil, trees, plants, and animals. These resources can last forever if used wisely.

Other natural resources will run out one day. These **nonrenewable resources** are resources that cannot be replaced. For example, coal formed over millions of years. Once we use the coal up, it is gone.

Managing Natural Resources

People need to manage natural resources to protect them for the future. Consider how your life might change if we ran out of forests, for example. Although forests are renewable, we can cut down trees far faster than they can grow. The result is the clearing of trees, or **deforestation**.

By managing resources, however, we can repair and prevent resource loss. For example, some groups are engaged in **reforestation**, planting trees to replace lost forestland.

READING CHECK Contrasting How do renewable and nonrenewable resources differ?

Energy Resources

Every day you use plants and animals from the dinosaur age—in the form of energy resources. These resources power vehicles, produce heat, and generate electricity. They are some of our most important and valuable natural resources.

Nonrenewable Energy Resources

Most of the energy we use comes from **fossil fuels**, nonrenewable resources that formed from the remains of ancient plants and animals. The most important fossil fuels are coal, petroleum, and natural gas.

Coal has long been a reliable energy source for heat. However, burning coal causes some problems. It pollutes the air and can harm the land. For these reasons, people have used coal less as other fuel options became available.

FOCUS ON READING

In the second sentence on this page, what cause does the word *because* signal? What is the effect of this cause?

Today we use coal mainly to create electricity at power plants, not to heat single buildings. Because coal is plentiful, people are looking for cleaner ways to burn it.

Petroleum, or oil, is a dark liquid used to make fuels and other products. When first removed from the ground, petroleum is called crude oil. This oil is shipped or piped to refineries, factories that process the crude oil to make products. Fuels made from oil include gasoline, diesel fuel, and jet fuel. Oil is also used to make petrochemicals, which are processed to make products such as plastics and cosmetics.

As with coal, burning oil-based fuels can pollute the air and land. In addition, oil spills can harm wildlife. Because we are so dependent on oil for energy, however, it is an extremely valuable resource.

The cleanest-burning fossil fuel is natural gas. We use it mainly for heating and cooking. For example, your kitchen stove may use natural gas. Some vehicles run on natural gas as well. These vehicles cause less pollution than those that run on gasoline.

Renewable Energy Resources

Unlike fossil fuels, renewable energy resources will not run out. They also are generally better for the environment. On the other hand, they are not available everywhere and can be costly.

The main alternative to fossil fuels is **hydroelectric power**—the production of electricity from waterpower. We obtain energy from moving water by damming rivers. The dams harness the power of moving water to generate electricity.

Hydroelectric power has both pros and cons. On the positive side, it produces power without polluting and lessens our use of fossil fuels. On the negative side, dams create lakes that replace existing resources, such as farmland, and disrupt wildlife habitats.

Another renewable energy source is wind. People have long used wind to power windmills. Today we use wind to power wind turbines, a type of modern windmill. At wind farms, hundreds of turbines create electricity in windy places.

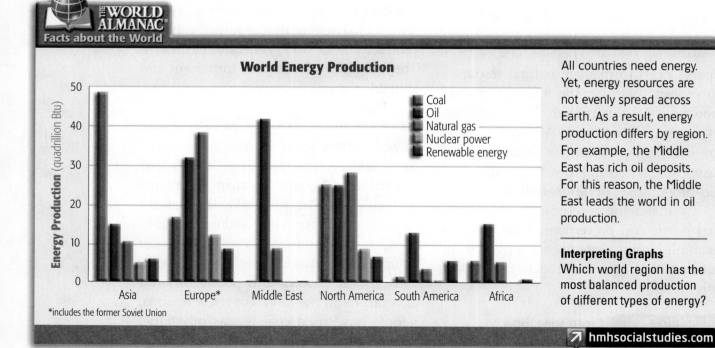

THE WORLD ALMANAC® Facts about the World

World Energy Production

Energy Production (quadrillion Btu)

Legend:
- Coal
- Oil
- Natural gas
- Nuclear power
- Renewable energy

Regions: Asia, Europe*, Middle East, North America, South America, Africa

*includes the former Soviet Union

All countries need energy. Yet, energy resources are not evenly spread across Earth. As a result, energy production differs by region. For example, the Middle East has rich oil deposits. For this reason, the Middle East leads the world in oil production.

Interpreting Graphs
Which world region has the most balanced production of different types of energy?

hmhsocialstudies.com

A third source of renewable energy is heat from the sun and Earth. We can use solar power, or power from the sun, to heat water or homes. Using special solar panels, we turn solar energy into electricity. We can also use geothermal energy, or heat from within Earth. Geothermal power plants use steam and hot water located within Earth to create electricity.

Nuclear Energy

A final energy source is nuclear energy. We obtain this energy by splitting atoms, small particles of matter. This process uses the metal uranium, so some people consider nuclear energy a nonrenewable resource. Nuclear power does not pollute the air, but it does produce dangerous wastes. These wastes must be stored for thousands of years before they are safe. In addition, an accident at a nuclear power plant can have terrible effects.

READING CHECK Drawing Inferences Why might people look for alternatives to fossil fuels?

Mineral Resources

Like energy resources, mineral resources can be quite valuable. These resources include metals, salt, rocks, and gemstones.

Minerals fulfill countless needs. Look around you to see a few. Your school building likely includes steel, made from iron. The outer walls might be granite or limestone. The window glass is made from quartz, a mineral in sand. From staples to jewelry to coins, metals are everywhere.

Minerals are nonrenewable, so we need to conserve them. Recycling items such as aluminum cans will make the supply of these valuable resources last longer.

READING CHECK Categorizing What are the major types of mineral resources?

From the Ground to the Air

The photo shows a bauxite mine. Bauxite is used to make aluminum. This metal is used in many products, such as jet planes. See how many other products made from aluminum you can name.

Resources and People

Natural resources vary from place to place. The resources available in a region can shape life and wealth for the people there.

Resources and Daily Life

The natural resources available to people affect their lifestyles and needs. In the United States we have many different kinds of natural resources. We can choose among many different ways to dress, eat, live, travel, and entertain ourselves. People in places with fewer natural resources will likely have fewer choices and different needs than Americans.

For example, people who live in remote rain forests depend on forest resources for most of their needs. These people may craft containers by weaving plant fibers together. They may make canoes by hollowing out tree trunks. Instead of being concerned about money, they might be more concerned about food.

Products from Petroleum

This Ohio family shows some common products made from petroleum, or oil.

ANALYZING VISUALS What petroleum-based products can you identify in this photo?

Resources and Wealth

The availability of natural resources affects countries' economies as well. For example, the many natural resources available in the United States have helped it become one of the world's wealthiest countries. In contrast, countries with few natural resources often have weak economies.

Some countries have one or two valuable resources but few others. For example, Saudi Arabia is rich in oil but lacks water for growing food. As a result, Saudi Arabia must use its oil profits to import food.

READING CHECK Identifying Cause and Effect How can having few natural resources affect life and wealth in a region or country?

SUMMARY AND PREVIEW You can see that Earth's natural resources have many uses. Important natural resources include air, water, soils, forests, fuels, and minerals. In the next chapter you will read about the world's people and cultures.

Section 4 Assessment

hmhsocialstudies.com
ONLINE QUIZ

Reviewing Ideas, Terms, and Places

1. **a. Define** What are **renewable resources** and **nonrenewable resources**?
   b. Explain Why is it important for people to manage Earth's natural resources?
   c. Develop What are some things you can do to help manage and conserve natural resources?
2. **a. Define** What are **fossil fuels**, and why are they significant?
   b. Summarize What are three examples of renewable energy resources?
   c. Predict How do you think life might change as we begin to run out of petroleum?
3. **a. Recall** What are the main types of mineral resources?
   b. Analyze What are some products that we get from mineral resources?

4. **a. Describe** How do resources affect people?
   b. Make Inferences How might a country with only one valuable resource develop its economy?

Critical Thinking

5. **Categorizing** Draw a chart like this one. Use your notes to identify and evaluate each energy resource.

Fossil Fuels	Renewable Energy	Nuclear Energy
Pros	Pros	Pros
Cons	Cons	Cons

FOCUS ON VIEWING

6. **Noting Details about Natural Resources** What natural resources does the place you chose have? Note ways to refer to some of these resources (or the lack of them) in your weather report.

from
The River

by Gary Paulsen

About the Reading *In the novel* The River, *a teenager named Brian has already proven his ability to survive in the wilderness. On this trip into the wilderness, he is accompanied by a man who wants to learn survival skills from him. With only a pocket knife and a transistor radio as tools, the two men meet challenges that at first appear too difficult to overcome. In the following passage from the novel, the men have just arrived in the wilderness.*

AS YOU READ Notice how Brian uses his senses to predict how some natural resources can help him survive.

He didn't just hear birds singing, not just a background sound of birds, but each bird. He listened to each bird. Located it, knew where it was by the sound, listened for the sound of alarm. He didn't just see clouds, but light clouds, scout clouds that came before the heavier clouds that could mean rain and maybe wind. ❶ The clouds were coming out of the northwest, and that meant that weather would come with them. Not could, but would. There would be rain. Tonight, late, there would be rain.

His eyes swept the clearing. . . There was a stump there that probably held grubs; hardwood there for a bow, and willows there for arrows; a game trail, . . . porcupines, raccoons, bear, wolves, moose, skunk would be moving on the trail and into the clearing. ❷ He flared his nostrils, smelled the air, pulled the air along the sides of his tongue in a hissing sound and tasted it, but there was nothing. Just summer smells. The tang of pines, soft air, some mustiness from rotting vegetation. No animals. ❸

GUIDED READING

WORD HELP

grubs soft, thick wormlike forms of insects
flared widened
tang sharp, biting smell
mustiness damp, stale smell

❶ Scout clouds are clouds that appear to be searching for other clouds to come.

❷ Brian notes that the stump likely holds grubs. He can eat the grubs for food.

❸ Brian does not smell any animals nearby.

Why might Brian want to know if animals are around?

Connecting Literature to Geography

1. **Predicting** Brian observes the clouds and can tell from their appearance and movement that rain is coming. What might be some ways that he can use his environment to prepare for the rain?

2. **Finding Main Ideas** The environment provides many resources that we can use, from wood to plants to animals. What resources does Brian identify around him that he can use to survive?

Social Studies Skills

Analyzing a Bar Graph

Learn

Bar graphs are drawings that use bars to show data in a clear, visual format. Use these guidelines to analyze bar graphs.

- Read the title to identify the graph's subject and purpose.

- Read the graph's other labels. Note what the graph is measuring and the units of measurement being used. For example, this bar graph is measuring precipitation by climate. The unit of measurement is inches. If the graph uses colors, note their purpose.

- Analyze and compare the data. As you do, note any increases or decreases and look for trends or changes over time.

This bar graph compares the average annual precipitation of six climate regions.

The height of each bar indicates the amount of precipitation.

This graph shows precipitation in inches.

The names of the climate regions appear across the bottom.

Practice

❶ On the bar graph above, which climate region has the highest average annual precipitation?

❷ Which two climate regions have about the same amount?

❸ Which climate region receives an average of between 50 and 75 inches of precipitation each year?

Apply

Examine the World Energy Production Today bar graph in Section 4. Then use the graph to answer the following questions.

1. Which region produces the most oil?

2. Which three regions produce little or no nuclear power?

3. Based on the graph, what type of energy resource do most Asian countries likely use?

Chapter Review

Geography's Impact
video series
Review the video to answer the closing question:
How are climate and weather different, and how does the influence they have differ?

Visual Summary

Use the visual summary below to help you review the main ideas of the chapter.

QUICK FACTS

Earth has a wide range of climates, which we identify by precipitation, temperature, and native plant life.

Plants, animals, and the environment are interconnected and affect one another in many ways.

Earth's valuable natural resources, such as air, water, forests, and minerals, have many uses and affect people's lives.

Reviewing Vocabulary, Terms, and Places

Unscramble each group of letters below to spell a term that matches the given definition.

1. **usumh**—decayed plant or animal matter

2. **tahrewe**—changes or conditions in the air at a certain time and place

3. **netorietfaosr**—planting trees where forests were

4. **neticxt**—completely died out

5. **estpep**—semidry grassland or prairie

6. **sifeticatorined**—spread of desertlike conditions

7. **laitemc**—an area's weather patterns over a long period of time

8. **arsmofrtpe**—permanently frozen layers of soil

9. **snonomo**—winds that change direction with the seasons and create wet and dry periods

10. **vansanas**—areas of tall grasses and scattered shrubs and trees

Comprehension and Critical Thinking

SECTION 1 *(Pages 50–54)*

11. a. **Identify** What five factors affect climate?

   b. **Analyze** Is average annual precipitation an example of weather or climate?

   c. **Evaluate** Of the five factors that affect climate, which one do you think is the most important? Why?

SECTION 2 *(Pages 55–61)*

12. a. **Recall** What are the five major climate zones?

   b. **Explain** How does latitude relate to climate?

   c. **Elaborate** Why do you think the study of climate is important in geography?

SECTION 3 *(Pages 62–65)*

13. a. **Define** What is an ecosystem, and why does it exist in a fragile balance?

SECTION 3 (continued)

b. Explain Why are plants an important part of the environment?

c. Predict What might be some results of desertification?

SECTION 4 (Pages 68–72)

14. a. Define What are minerals?

b. Contrast How do nonrenewable resources and renewable resources differ?

c. Elaborate How might a scarcity of natural resources affect life in a region?

Using the Internet 21ST CENTURY

15. Activity: Experiencing Extremes Could you live in a place where for part of the year it is always dark and temperatures plummet to –104°F? What if you had to live in a place where it is always wet and stormy? Through your online textbook, learn more about some of the world's extreme climates. Then create a poster that describes some of those climates and the people, animals, and plants that live in them.

hmhsocialstudies.com

Social Studies Skills

Analyzing a Bar Graph *Examine the bar graph titled Average Annual Precipitation by Climate Region in the Social Studies Skills for this chapter. Then use the bar graph to answer the following questions.*

16. Which climate region receives an average of 100 inches of precipitation a year?

17. Which climate region receives an average of 25 inches of precipitation a year?

18. What is the difference in average annual precipitation between tropical humid climates and Mediterranean climates?

Map Activity 21ST CENTURY

19. Prevailing Winds On a separate sheet of paper, match the letters on the map with their correct labels.

equator   South Pole   westerly
North Pole   trade wind

hmhsocialstudies.com **INTERACTIVE MAP**

map zone

→ Cool air
→ Warm air
→ Wind direction

FOCUS ON READING AND VIEWING

Understanding Cause and Effect *Answer the following questions about causes and effects.*

20. What causes desertification?

21. What are the effects of abundant natural resources on a country's economy?

22. Presenting and Viewing a Weather Report Select a place and a season to write a weather report about. Describe the weather and predict upcoming weather. Present your report to your class. Use a professional, friendly tone of voice and make frequent eye contact with your audience. Then view your classmates' weather reports. Be prepared to give feedback on the content and their presentation techniques.

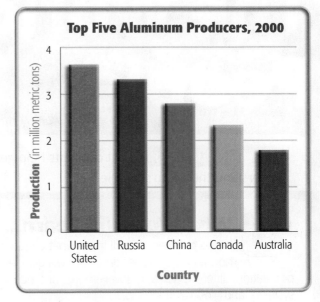

Standardized Test Prep

CHAPTER 3

DIRECTIONS: Read questions 1 through 7 and write the letter of the best response. Then read question 8 and write your own well-constructed response.

1 The cold winds that flow away from the North and South poles are the
A doldrums.
B polar easterlies.
C trade winds.
D westerlies.

2 Which climate zone occurs only in the upper latitudes?
A highland
B temperate
C tropical
D polar

3 Where are the most diverse habitats on Earth found?
A steppe
B tropical rain forest
C tropical savanna
D tundra

4 What is the cleanest burning fossil fuel?
A coal
B natural gas
C oil
D petroleum

5 Which renewable energy source uses the heat of Earth's interior to generate power?
A geothermal energy
B hydroelectric energy
C nuclear energy
D solar energy

6 Based on the graph above, which country produced about 2.8 million tons of aluminum in 2000?
A Australia
B China
C Russia
D United States

7 Which of the following form over tropical waters and are Earth's largest and most destructive storms?
A blizzards
B hurricanes
C thunderstorms
D tornadoes

8 Extended Response Forces such as the sun, latitude, wind, and water shape climate. Examine the World Climate Regions map in Section 2. Describe two climate patterns that you see on the map and explain how various forces combine to create the two patterns.

The World's People

Essential Question What concepts help geographers understand the world's people?

What You Will Learn...

In this chapter you will learn what culture is and how it changes over time. You will also learn about population, different types of governments and economic systems, and globalization.

FOCUS ON READING AND WRITING

Understanding Main Ideas A main idea is the central idea around which a paragraph or passage is organized. As you read, ask yourself what each paragraph is about. Look for a sentence or two that summarizes the main point of the entire paragraph. **See the lesson, Understanding Main Ideas, on page 109.**

Creating a Poster Think of some great posters you have seen at the movies, in bus stations, or in the halls of your school. They likely all had a colorful image that captured your attention and a few words that explained the main idea. Read this chapter about the world's people. Then create a poster that includes words and images that summarize the chapter's main ideas.

Culture Thousands of different cultures make up our world. Clothing, language, and music are just some parts of culture.

Many of the world's people come together every four years to compete in the Olympics.

What indicates that some of the people in this photo are from different parts of the world?

Population Geographers study human populations like this one in India to learn where and why people live in certain places.

Global Connections Technology allows people in remote places around the world to communicate.

Culture

If YOU lived there...

You live in New York City, and your young cousin from out of state has come to visit. As you take her on a tour of the city, you point out the different cultural neighborhoods, like Chinatown, Little Italy, Spanish Harlem, and Koreatown. Your cousin isn't quite sure what culture means or why these neighborhoods are so different.

How can you explain what culture is?

What You Will Learn...

Main Ideas

1. Culture is the set of beliefs, goals, and practices that a group of people share.
2. The world includes many different culture groups.
3. New ideas and events lead to changes in culture.

The Big Idea

Culture, a group's shared practices and beliefs, differs from group to group and changes over time.

Key Terms

culture, *p. 80*
culture trait, *p. 81*
culture region, *p. 82*
ethnic group, *p. 83*
cultural diversity, *p. 83*
cultural diffusion, *p. 85*

hmhsocialstudies.com
TAKING NOTES

Use the graphic organizer online to take notes on culture.

What Is Culture?

If you traveled around the world, you would experience many different sights and sounds. You would probably hear unique music, eat a variety of foods, listen to different languages, see distinctive landscapes, and learn new customs. You would see and take part in the variety of cultures that exist in our world.

A Way of Life

What exactly is culture? **Culture** is the set of beliefs, values, and practices that a group of people has in common. Culture includes many aspects of life, such as language and religion, that we may share with people around us. Everything in your day-to-day life is part of your culture, from the clothes you wear to the music you hear to the foods you eat.

On your world travels, you might notice that all societies share certain cultural features. All people have some kind of government, educate their children in some way, and create some type of art or music. However, not all societies practice their culture in the same way. For example, in Japan the school year begins in the spring, and students wear school uniforms. In the United States, however, the school year begins in the late

Culture Traits

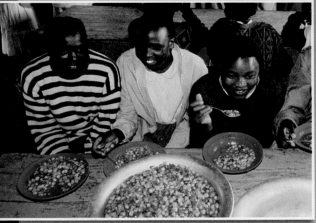

These students in Japan and Kenya have some culture traits in common, like eating lunch at school. Other culture traits are different.

ANALYZING VISUALS What culture traits do these students share? Which are different?

summer, and most schools do not require uniforms. Differences like these are what make each culture unique.

Culture Traits

Cultural features like starting the school year in the spring or wearing uniforms are types of culture traits. A **culture trait** is an activity or behavior in which people often take part. The language you speak and the sports you play are some of your culture traits. Sometimes a culture trait is shared by people around the world. For example, all around the globe people participate in the game of soccer. In places as different as Germany, Nigeria, and Saudi Arabia, many people enjoy playing and watching soccer.

While some culture traits are shared around the world, others change from place to place. One example of this is how people around the world eat. In China most people use chopsticks to eat their food. In Europe, however, people use forks and spoons. In Ethiopia, many people use bread or their fingers to scoop their food.

Development of Culture

How do cultures develop? Culture traits are often learned or passed down from one generation to the next. Most culture traits develop within families as traditions, foods, or holiday customs are handed down over the years. Laws and moral codes are also passed down within societies. Many laws in the United States, for example, can be traced back to England in the 1600s and were brought by colonists to America.

Cultures also develop as people learn new culture traits. Immigrants who move to a new country, for example, might learn to speak the language or eat the foods of their adopted country.

Other factors, such as history and the environment, also affect how cultures develop. For example, historical events changed the language and religion of much of Central and South America. In the 1500s, when the Spanish conquered the region, they introduced their language and Roman Catholic faith. The environment in which we live can also shape culture.

FOCUS ON READING
What is the main idea of this paragraph?

For example, the desert environment of Africa's Sahara influences the way people who live there earn a living. Rather than grow crops, they herd animals that have adapted to the harsh environment. As you can see, history and the environment affect how cultures develop.

READING CHECK **Finding Main Ideas** What practices and customs make up culture?

Culture Groups

Earth is home to thousands of different cultures. People who share similar culture traits are members of the same culture group. Culture groups can be based on a variety of factors, such as age, language, or religion. American teenagers, for example, can be said to form a culture group based on location and age. They share similar tastes in music, clothing, and sports.

Culture Regions

When we refer to culture groups, we are speaking of people who share a common culture. At other times, however, we need to refer to the area, or region, where the culture group is found. A **culture region** is an area in which people have many shared culture traits.

In a specific culture region, people share certain culture traits, such as religious beliefs, language, or lifestyle. One well-known culture region is the Arab world. As you can see at right, an Arab culture region spreads across Southwest Asia and North Africa. In this region, most people write and speak Arabic and are Muslim. They also share other traits, such as foods, music, styles of clothing, and architecture.

Occasionally, a single culture region dominates an entire country. In Japan, for example, one primary culture dominates the country. Nearly everyone in Japan speaks the same language and follows the same practices. Many Japanese bow to their elders as a sign of respect and remove their shoes when they enter a home.

A single country may also include more than one culture region within its borders. Mexico is one of many countries that is made up of different culture regions. People in northern Mexico and southern Mexico, for example, have different culture traits. The culture of northern Mexico tends to be more modern, while traditional culture remains strong in southern Mexico.

A culture region may also stretch across country borders. As you have already learned, an Arab culture region dominates much of Southwest Asia and North Africa. Another example is the Kurdish culture region, home to the Kurds, a people that live throughout Turkey, Iran, and Iraq.

Arab Culture Region

Culture regions are based on shared culture traits. Southwest Asia and North Africa make up an Arab culture region based on ethnic heritage, a common language, and religion. Most people in this region are Arab, speak and write Arabic, and practice Islam.

Cultural Diversity

As you just learned, countries may contain several culture regions within their borders. Often, these culture regions are based on ethnic groups. An **ethnic group** is a group of people who share a common culture and ancestry. Members of ethnic groups often share certain culture traits such as religion, language, and even special foods.

Some countries are home to a variety of ethnic groups. For example, more than 100 different ethnic groups live in the East African country of Tanzania. Countries with many ethnic groups are culturally diverse. **Cultural diversity** is the state of having a variety of cultures in the same area. While cultural diversity creates an interesting mix of ideas, behaviors, and practices, it can also lead to conflict.

In some countries, ethnic groups have been in conflict. In Canada, for example, some French Canadians want to separate from the rest of Canada to preserve their language and culture. In the 1990s ethnic conflict in the African country of Rwanda led to extreme violence and bloodshed.

Although ethnic groups have clashed in some culturally diverse countries, they have cooperated in others. In the United States, for example, many different ethnic groups live side by side. Cities and towns often celebrate their ethnic heritage with festivals and parades, like the Saint Patrick's Day Parade in Boston or Philadelphia's Puerto Rican Festival.

READING CHECK **Making Inferences** Why might cultural diversity cause conflict?

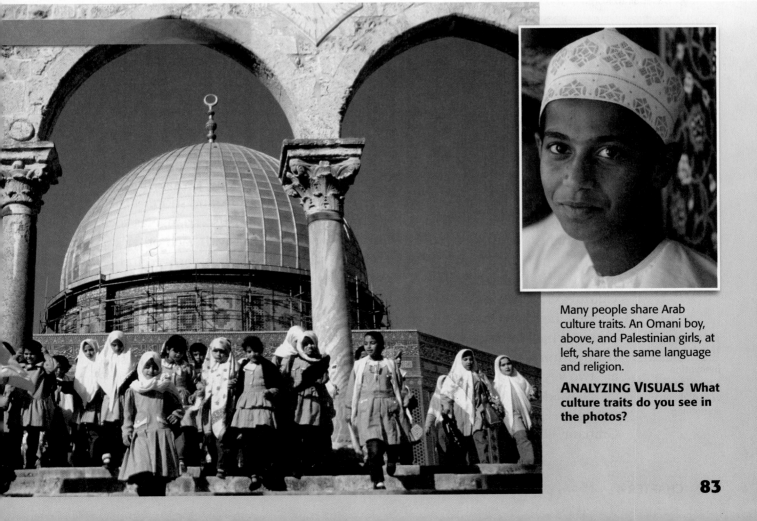

Many people share Arab culture traits. An Omani boy, above, and Palestinian girls, at left, share the same language and religion.

ANALYZING VISUALS What culture traits do you see in the photos?

Cultural Diffusion of Baseball

Like many other ideas and customs, baseball has spread around the world through the process of cultural diffusion. Since its beginnings in New York in the 1800s, baseball has spread throughout the United States, into Central and South America, and to Asia.

Spread of baseball

0   1,000   2,000 Miles
0   1,000 2,000 Kilometers
Projection: Miller Cylindrical

NORTH AMERICA

ASIA

PACIFIC OCEAN

UNITED STATES

New York
Origin of baseball

ATLANTIC OCEAN

SOUTH AMERICA

American missionaries introduced baseball to Korea in 1905.

American students first brought baseball to Cuba in the 1800s.

Changes in Culture

You've read books or seen movies set in the time of the Civil War or in the Wild West of the late 1800s. Think about how our culture has changed since then. Clothing, food, music—all have changed drastically. When we study cultural change, we try to find out what caused the changes and how those changes spread from place to place.

How Cultures Change

Cultures change constantly. Some changes happen rapidly, while others take many years. What causes cultures to change? **Innovation** and contact with other people are two key causes of cultural change.

New ideas often bring about cultural changes. For example, when Alexander Graham Bell invented the telephone, it changed how people communicate with each other. Other innovations, such as motion pictures, changed how people spend their free time. More recently, the creation of the Internet dramatically altered the way people find information, communicate, and shop.

Cultures also change as societies come into contact with each other. For example, when the Spanish arrived in the Americas, they introduced firearms and horses to the region, changing the lifestyle of some Native American groups. At the same time, the Spaniards learned about new foods like potatoes and chocolate. These foods then became an important part of Europeans' diet. The Chinese had a similar influence on Korea and Japan, where they introduced Buddhism and written language.

ACADEMIC VOCABULARY

innovation a new idea or way of doing something

Organized baseball began in New York around 1845 and quickly spread around the world.

Where did baseball begin, and to what parts of the world did it eventually spread?

How Ideas Spread

You have probably noticed that a new slang word might spread from teenager to teenager and state to state. In the same way, clothing styles from New York or Paris might become popular all over the world. More serious cultural traits spread as well. Religious beliefs or ideas about government may spread from place to place. The spread of culture traits from one region to another is called **cultural diffusion**.

Cultural diffusion often occurs when people move from one place to another. For example, when Europeans settled in the Americas, they brought their culture along with them. As a result, English, French, Spanish, and Portuguese are all spoken in the Americas. American culture also spread as pioneers moved west, taking with them their form of government, religious beliefs, and customs.

Cultural diffusion also takes place as new ideas spread from place to place. As you can see on the map above, the game of baseball first began in New York, then spread throughout the United States. As more and more people learned the game, it spread even faster and farther. Baseball eventually spread around the world. Wearing blue jeans became part of our culture in a similar way. Blue jeans originated in the American West in the mid-1800s. They gradually became popular all over the country and the world.

READING CHECK Finding Main Ideas How do cultures change over time?

SUMMARY AND PREVIEW In this section you learned about the role that culture plays in our lives and how our cultures change. Next, you will learn about human populations and how we keep track of Earth's changing population.

Section 1 Assessment

hmhsocialstudies.com
ONLINE QUIZ

Reviewing Ideas, Terms, and Places
1. a. **Define** What is **culture**?
   b. **Analyze** What influences the development of culture?
   c. **Elaborate** How might the world be different if we all shared the same culture?
2. a. **Identify** What are the different types of **culture regions**?
   b. **Analyze** How does **cultural diversity** affect societies?
3. a. **Describe** How does **cultural diffusion** take place?
   b. **Make Inferences** How can the spread of new ideas lead to cultural change?
   c. **Evaluate** Do you think that cultural diffusion has a positive or a negative effect? Explain your answer.

Critical Thinking
4. **Finding Main Ideas** Using your notes and a chart like the one here, explain the main idea of each aspect of culture in your own words.

Culture Traits	Culture Groups	Cultural Change

FOCUS ON WRITING

5. **Writing about Culture** What key words about culture can you include on your poster? What images might you include? Jot down your ideas in your notebook.

Population

If YOU lived there...

You live in Mexico City, one of the largest and most crowded cities in the world. You realize just how crowded it is whenever you ride the subway at rush hour! You love the excitement of living in a big city. There is always something interesting to do. At the same time, the city has a lot of crime. Heavy traffic pollutes the air.

What do you like and dislike about living in a large city?

What You Will Learn...

Main Ideas

1. The study of population patterns helps geographers learn about the world.
2. Population statistics and trends are important measures of population change.

The Big Idea

Population studies are an important part of geography.

Key Terms

population, *p. 86*
population density, *p. 86*
birthrate, *p. 88*
migration, *p. 89*

hmhsocialstudies.com
TAKING NOTES

Use the graphic organizer online to take notes on population.

BUILDING BACKGROUND An important part of geographers' work is the study of human populations. Many geographers are interested in where people live, how many people live there, and what effects those people have on resources and the environment.

Population Patterns

How many people live in your community? Do you live in a small town, a huge city, or somewhere in between? Your community's **population**, or the total number of people in a given area, determines a great deal about the place in which you live. Population influences the variety of businesses, the types of transportation, and the number of schools in your community.

Because population has a huge impact on our lives, it is an important part of geography. Geographers who study human populations are particularly interested in patterns that emerge over time. They study such information as how many people live in an area, why people live where they do, and how populations change. Population patterns like these can tell us much about our world.

Population Density

Some places on Earth are crowded with people. Others are almost empty. One statistic geographers use to examine populations is **population density**, a measure of the number of people living in an area. Population density is expressed as persons per square mile or square kilometer.

World Population Density

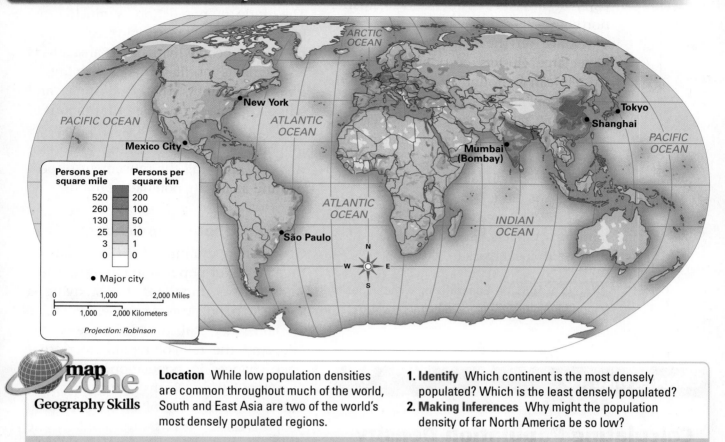

Persons per square mile | **Persons per square km**
520 | 200
260 | 100
130 | 50
25 | 10
3 | 1
0 | 0

● Major city

0   1,000   2,000 Miles
0 1,000 2,000 Kilometers

Projection: Robinson

map zone
Geography Skills

Location While low population densities are common throughout much of the world, South and East Asia are two of the world's most densely populated regions.

1. **Identify** Which continent is the most densely populated? Which is the least densely populated?
2. **Making Inferences** Why might the population density of far North America be so low?

Population density provides us with important information about a place. The more people per square mile in a region, the more crowded, or dense, it is. Japan, for example, has a population density of 880 people per square mile (340 per square km). That is a high population density. In many parts of Japan, people are crowded together in large cities, and space is very limited. In contrast, Australia has a very low population density. Only 6 people per square mile (2 per square km) live there. Australia has many wide-open spaces with very few people.

How do you think population density affects life in a particular place? In places with high population densities, the land is often expensive, roads are crowded, and buildings tend to be taller. On the other hand, places with low population densities tend to have more open spaces, less traffic, and more available land.

Where People Live

Can you tell where most of the world's people live by examining the population density map above? The reds and purples on the map indicate areas of very high population density, while the light yellow areas indicate sparse populations. When an area is thinly populated, it is often because the land does not provide a very good life. These areas may have rugged mountains or harsh deserts where people cannot grow crops. Some areas may be frozen all year long, making survival there very difficult.

↗ hmhsocialstudies.com
ANIMATED GEOGRAPHY
Earth at Night

For these reasons, very few people live in parts of far North America, Greenland, northern Asia, and Australia.

Notice on the map that some areas have large clusters of population. Such clusters can be found in East and South Asia, Europe, and eastern North America. Fertile soil, reliable sources of water, and a good agricultural climate make these good regions for settlement. For example, the North China Plain in East Asia is one of the most densely populated regions in the world. The area's plentiful agricultural land, many rivers, and mild climate have made it an ideal place to settle.

READING CHECK **Generalizing** What types of information can population density provide?

CONNECTING TO Math

Calculating Population Density

Population density measures the number of people living in an area. To calculate population density, divide a place's total population by its area in square miles (or square kilometers). For example, if your city has a population of 100,000 people and an area of 100 square miles, you would divide 100,000 by 100. This would give you a population density of 1,000 people per square mile ($100,000 \div 100 = 1,000$).

Analyzing If a city had a population of 615,000 and a total land area of 250 square miles, what would its population density be?

City	Population	Total Area (square miles)	Population Density (people per square mile)
Adelaide, Australia	1,145,000	336	3,408
Lima, Peru	8,012,000	1,029	7,786
Nairobi, Kenya	3,010,000	266	11,316

Population Change

The study of population is much more important than you might realize. The number of people living in an area affects all elements of life—the availability of housing and jobs, whether hospitals and schools open or close, even the amount of available food. Geographers track changes in populations by examining important statistics, studying the movement of people, and analyzing population trends.

Tracking Population Changes

Geographers examine three key statistics to learn about population changes. These statistics are important for studying a country's population over time.

Three key statistics—birthrate, death rate, and the rate of natural increase—track changes in population. Births add to a population. Deaths subtract from it. The annual number of births per 1,000 people is called the **birthrate**. Similarly, the death rate is the annual number of deaths per 1,000 people. The birthrate minus the death rate equals the percentage of natural increase, or the rate at which a population is changing. For example, Denmark has a rate of natural increase of 0.05%. This means it has slightly more births than deaths and a very slight population increase.

Population growth rates differ from one place to another. In some countries, populations are growing very slowly or even shrinking. Many countries in Europe and North America have very low rates of natural increase. In Russia, for example, the birthrate is about 10.8 and the death rate is 16.1. The result is a negative rate of natural increase and a shrinking population.

In most countries around the world, however, populations are growing. Mali, for example, has a rate of natural increase of about 3.3 percent. While that may sound

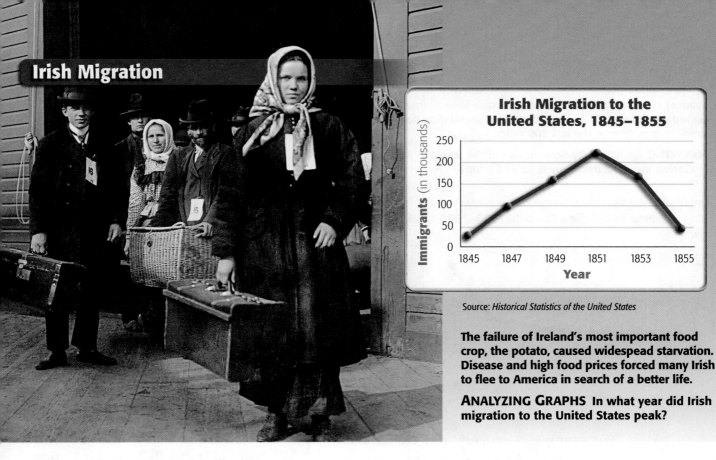

Irish Migration

Irish Migration to the United States, 1845–1855

Source: *Historical Statistics of the United States*

The failure of Ireland's most important food crop, the potato, caused widespead starvation. Disease and high food prices forced many Irish to flee to America in search of a better life.

ANALYZING GRAPHS In what year did Irish migration to the United States peak?

small, it means that Mali's population is expected to double in only 21 years! High population growth rates can pose some challenges, as governments try to provide enough jobs, education, and medical care for their rapidly growing populations.

Migration

A common cause of population change is migration. **Migration** is the process of moving from one place to live in another. As one country loses citizens as a result of migration, its population can decline. At the same time, another country may gain population as people settle there.

People migrate for many reasons. Some factors push people to leave their country, while other factors pull, or attract, people to new countries. Warfare, a lack of jobs, or a lack of good farmland are common push factors. For example, during the Irish potato famine of the mid-1800s, poverty and disease forced some 1.5 million people to leave Ireland. Opportunities for a better life often pull people to new countries. For example, in the 1800s and early 1900s thousands of British citizens migrated to Australia in search of cheap land.

World Population Trends

In the last 200 years Earth's population has exploded. For thousands of years world population growth was low and relatively steady. About 2,000 years ago, the world had some 300 million people. By 1800 there were almost 1 billion people. Since 1800, better health care and improved food production have supported tremendous population growth. In 2012 the world's population passed 7 billion people.

Population trends are an important part of the study of the world's people. Two important population trends are clear today. The first trend indicates that the population growth in some of the more industrialized nations has begun to slow.

FOCUS ON READING

What is the main idea of this paragraph? What facts are used to support that idea?

World Population Growth

Advances in food production and health care have dramatically lowered death rates. As a result, the global population has seen incredible growth over the last 200 years.

ANALYZING GRAPHS By how much did the world's population increase between 1800 and 2000?

World Population Growth, 1500–2000

(y-axis: Population (in billions), values 0, 2, 4, 6, 8)
(x-axis: Year — 1500, 1600, 1700, 1800, 1900, 2000)

Source: *Atlas of World Population History*

For example, Germany and France have low rates of natural increase. A second trend indicates that less industrialized countries, like Nigeria and Bangladesh, often have high growth rates. These trends affect a country's workforce and government aid.

READING CHECK **Summarizing** What population statistics do geographers study? Why?

SUMMARY AND PREVIEW In this section you have learned where people live, how crowded places are, and how population affects our world. Geographers study past and present population patterns in order to plan for the future. In the next section, you will learn how governments and economies affect people on Earth.

Section 2 Assessment

hmhsocialstudies.com
ONLINE QUIZ

Reviewing Ideas, Terms, and Places

1. **a. Identify** What regions of the world have the highest levels of **population density**?
   b. Draw Conclusions What information can be learned by studying population density?
   c. Evaluate Would you prefer to live in a region with a dense or a sparse population? Why?
2. **a. Describe** What is natural increase? What can it tell us about a country?
   b. Analyze What effect does **migration** have on human populations?
   c. Predict What patterns do you think world population might have in the future?

Critical Thinking

3. **Summarizing** Draw a graphic organizer like the one here. Use your notes to write a sentence that summarizes each aspect of the study of population.

Population Patterns

Population Change

FOCUS ON WRITING

4. **Discussing Population** What effect does population have on our world? Write down some words and phrases that you might use on your poster to explain the importance of population.

Government and Economy

If YOU were there...

You live in Raleigh, North Carolina. Your class at school is planning a presentation about life in the United States for a group of visitors from Japan. Your teacher wants you to discuss government and economics in the United States. As you prepare for your speech, you wonder what you should say.

How do government and economics affect your life?

BUILDING BACKGROUND Although you probably don't think about them every day, your country's government and economy have a big influence on your life. That is true in every country in every part of the world. Governments and economic systems affect everything from a person's rights to the type of job he or she has.

Governments of the World

Can you imagine what life would be like if there were no rules? Without ways to establish order and ensure justice, life would be chaotic. That explains why societies have governments. Our governments make and enforce laws, regulate business and trade, and provide aid to people. Governments help shape the culture and economy of a country as well as the daily lives of the people who live there.

Democratic Governments

Many countries—including the United States, Canada, and Mexico—have democratic governments. A **democracy** is a form of government in which the people elect leaders and rule by majority. In most democratic countries, citizens are free to choose representatives to make and enforce the laws. Voters in the United States, for example, elect members of Congress, who make the laws, and the president, who enforces those laws.

What You Will Learn...

Main Ideas

1. The governments of the world include democracy, monarchy, dictatorship, and communism.
2. Different economic activities and systems exist throughout the world.
3. Geographers group the countries of the world based on their level of economic development.

The Big Idea

The world's countries have different governments and levels of economic development.

Key Terms

democracy, *p. 91*
communism, *p. 92*
market economy, *p. 94*
command economy, *p. 94*
gross domestic product (GDP), *p. 95*
developed countries, *p. 95*
developing countries, *p. 95*

hmhsocialstudies.com
TAKING NOTES

Use the graphic organizer online to take notes on different types of governments and economies.

THE WORLD'S PEOPLE **91**

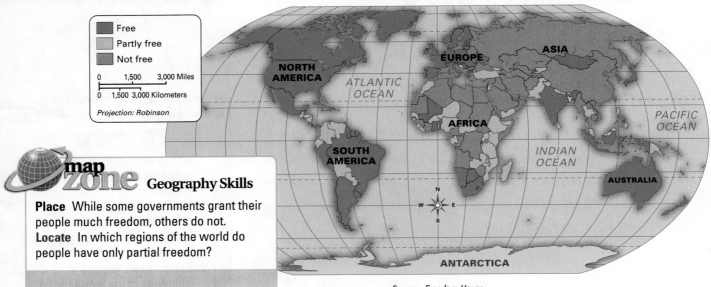

Free
Partly free
Not free

0   1,500   3,000 Miles
0 1,500 3,000 Kilometers

Projection: Robinson

NORTH AMERICA
ATLANTIC OCEAN
EUROPE
ASIA
AFRICA
SOUTH AMERICA
INDIAN OCEAN
PACIFIC OCEAN
AUSTRALIA
ANTARCTICA

map zone Geography Skills

Place While some governments grant their people much freedom, others do not.
Locate In which regions of the world do people have only partial freedom?

Source: *Freedom House*

FOCUS ON READING

Main ideas are not always stated in the first sentence. Which sentence in this paragraph states the main idea?

Most democratic governments in the world work to protect the freedoms and rights of their people, such as the freedom of speech and the freedom of religion. Other democracies, however, restrict the rights and freedoms of their people. Not all democratic governments in the world are completely free.

Other Types of Government

Not all of the world's countries, however, are democracies. Several other types of government are found in the world today, including monarchies, dictatorships, and Communist states.

Monarchy is one of the oldest types of government in the world. A monarchy is ruled directly by a king or queen, the head of a royal family. Saudi Arabia is an example of a monarchy. The Saudi king has executive, legislative, and judicial powers. In some monarchies, power is in the hands of just one person. As a result, the people have little say in their government. Other monarchies, however, like Norway and Spain, use many democratic practices.

Dictatorship is a type of government in which a single, powerful ruler has total control. This leader, called a dictator, often rules by force. Iraq under Saddam Hussein was an example of a dictatorship. People who live under a dictatorship are not free. They have few rights and no say in their own government.

Yet another form of government is communism. **Communism** is a political system in which the government owns all property and dominates all aspects of life in a country. Leaders of most Communist governments are not elected by citizens. Rather, they are chosen by the Communist Party or by Communist leaders. In most Communist states, like Cuba and North Korea, the government strictly controls the country's economy and the daily life of its people. As a result, people in Communist states often have restricted rights and very little freedom.

READING CHECK **Supporting a Point of View** Why might people prefer to live in a democracy as opposed to a dictatorship?

Economies of the World

One important function of government is to monitor a country's economy. The economy is a system that includes all of the activities that people and businesses do to earn a living. Countries today use a mix of different economic activities and systems.

Economic Activity

Every country has some level of economic activity. Economic activities are ways in which people make a living. Some people farm, others manufacture goods, while still others provide services, such as driving a taxi or designing skyscrapers. Geographers divide these economic activities into four different levels.

The first level of economic activity, the primary industry, uses natural resources or raw materials. People in these industries earn a living by providing raw materials to others. Farming, fishing, and mining are all examples of primary industries. These activities provide raw materials such as grain, seafood, and coal for others to use.

Secondary industries perform the next step. They use natural resources or raw materials to manufacture other products. Manufacturing is the process in which raw materials are changed into finished goods. For example, people who make furniture might take wood and make products such as tables, chairs, or desks. Automobile manufacturers use steel, plastic, glass, and rubber to put together trucks and cars.

In the third level of activity, or tertiary industry, goods and services are exchanged. People in tertiary industries sell the furniture, automobiles, or other products made in secondary industries. Other people, like health care workers or mechanics, provide services rather than goods. Teachers, store clerks, doctors, and TV personalities are all engaged in this level of economic activity.

Economic Activity

Primary Industry

Primary industries use natural resources to make money. Here a farmer sells milk from dairy cows to earn a living.

Secondary Industry

Secondary economic activities use raw materials to produce or manufacture something new. In this case, the milk from dairy cows is used to make cheese.

Tertiary Industry

Tertiary economic activities provide services to people and businesses. This grocer selling cheese in a market is involved in a tertiary activity.

Quaternary Industry

Quaternary industries process and distribute information. Skilled workers research and gather information. Here, inspectors examine and test the quality of cheese.

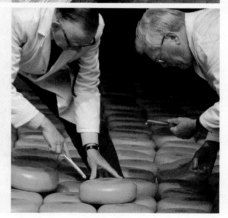

The highest level of economic activity, quaternary industry, involves the research and distribution of information. People making a living at this level work with information rather than goods, and often have specialized knowledge and skills. Architects, lawyers, and scientists all work in quaternary industries.

Economic Systems

Just as economic activities are organized into different types, so are our economic systems. Economic systems can be divided into three types: traditional, market, and command. Most countries today use a mix of these economic systems.

ACADEMIC
VOCABULARY
traditional
customary,
time-honored

One economic system is a **traditional** economy, a system in which people grow their own food and make their own goods. Trade may take place through barter, or the exchange of goods without the use of money. Rural and remote communities often have a mostly traditional economy.

The most common economic system used around the world today is a market economy. A **market economy** is a system based on private ownership, free trade, and competition. Individuals and businesses are free to buy and sell what they wish. Prices are determined by the supply and demand for goods. This is sometimes called capitalism. The United States is one of many countries that use this system.

A third system is a **command economy**, a system in which the central government makes all economic decisions. The government decides what goods to produce, how much to produce, and what prices will be. While no country has a purely command economy, the economies of North Korea and Cuba are close to it. The Communist governments of these nations own and control most businesses.

READING CHECK **Summarizing** What economic systems are used in the world today?

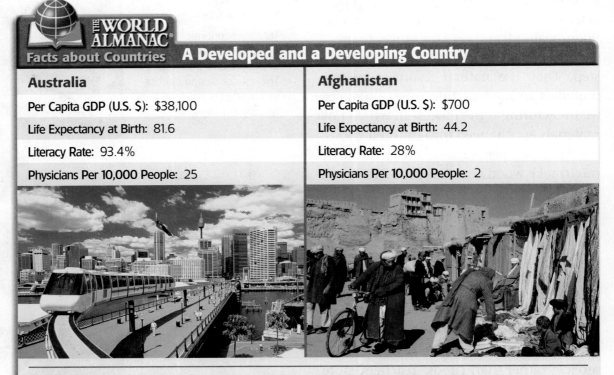

THE WORLD ALMANAC
Facts about Countries   A Developed and a Developing Country

Australia	Afghanistan
Per Capita GDP (U.S. $): $38,100	Per Capita GDP (U.S. $): $700
Life Expectancy at Birth: 81.6	Life Expectancy at Birth: 44.2
Literacy Rate: 93.4%	Literacy Rate: 28%
Physicians Per 10,000 People: 25	Physicians Per 10,000 People: 2

Contrasting How does the quality of life in Afghanistan differ from that in Australia?

hmhsocialstudies.com

Economic Development

Economic systems and activities affect a country's economic development, or the level of economic growth and quality of life. Geographers often group countries into two basic categories—developed and developing countries—based on their level of economic development.

Economic Indicators

Geographers use economic indicators, or measures of a country's wealth, to decide if a country is developed or developing. One such measure is gross domestic product. **Gross domestic product (GDP)** is the value of all goods and services produced within a country in a single year. Another indicator is a country's per capita GDP, or the total GDP divided by the number of people in a country. As you can see in the chart, per capita GDP allows us to compare incomes among countries. Other indicators include the level of industrialization and overall quality of life. In other words, we look at the types of industries and technology a country has, in addition to its level of health care and education.

Developed and Developing Countries

Many of the world's wealthiest and most powerful nations are **developed countries**, countries with strong economies and a high quality of life. Developed countries like Germany and the United States have a high per capita GDP and high levels of industrialization. Their health care and education systems are among the best in the world. Many people in developed countries have access to technology.

The world's poorer nations are known as **developing countries**, countries with less productive economies and a lower quality of life. Almost two-thirds of the people in the world live in developing countries. These developing countries have a lower per capita GDP than developed countries. Most of their citizens work in farming or other primary industries. Although these countries typically have large cities, much of their population still lives in rural areas. People in developing countries usually have less access to health care or technology. Guatemala, Nigeria, and Afghanistan are all developing countries.

READING CHECK **Analyzing** What factors separate developed and developing countries?

SUMMARY AND PREVIEW The world's countries have different governments, economies, and levels of development. Next, you will learn how people are linked in a global community.

Section 3 Assessment

hmhsocialstudies.com
ONLINE QUIZ

Reviewing Ideas, Terms, and Places

1. **a. Identify** What are some different types of government?
   b. Elaborate Under which type of government would you most want to live? Why?
2. **a. Describe** What are the levels of economic activity?
   b. Evaluate Which economic system do you think is best? Explain your answer.
3. **a. Define** What is **gross domestic product**?
   b. Contrast In what ways do **developed countries** differ from **developing countries**?

Critical Thinking

4. **Categorizing** Draw a chart like the one here. Use the chart and your notes to identify the different governments, economies, and levels of economic development in the world today.

Types of Government	Economic Systems	Economic Development

FOCUS ON WRITING

5. **Thinking about Government and Economy** What kinds of images and words could you use to present the main ideas behind the world's governments and economies?

Organizing Information

Learn

Remembering new information is easier if you organize it clearly. As you read and study, try to organize what you are learning. One way to do this is to create a graphic organizer. Follow these steps to create a graphic organizer as you read.

- Identify the main idea of the passage. Write the main idea in a circle at the top of your page.
- As you read, look for subtopics under the main idea. On your paper, draw a row of circles below the main idea, one for each subtopic. Write the subtopics in the circles.
- Below each subtopic, draw a big box. Look for facts and supporting details for each subtopic. List them in the box below the subtopic.

Practice

Read the passage below carefully. Then use the graphic organizer above to organize the information from the passage.

> Cultures change slowly over time. New ideas and new people can often lead to cultural change.
>
> Cultures often change as new ideas are introduced to a society. New ways of doing things, new inventions, and even new beliefs can all change a culture. One example of this is the spread of computer technology. As people adopted computers, they learned a new language and new work habits.
>
> Cultures also change when new people introduce their culture traits to a society. For example, as immigrants settle in the United States, they add new culture traits, like food, music, and clothing, to American culture.

Apply

Turn to Section 1 and read the passage titled Culture Regions. Draw a graphic organizer like the one above. Then follow the steps to organize the information you have read. The passage will have two or more subtopics. Add additional circles and rectangles for each additional subtopic you find.

Global Connections

If YOU lived there...

You live in Louisville, Kentucky, and you have never traveled out of the United States. However, when you got ready for school this morning, you put on a T-shirt made in Guatemala and jeans made in Malaysia. Your shoes came from China. You rode to school on a bus with parts manufactured in Mexico. At school, your class even took part in a discussion with students in Canada.

What makes your global connections possible?

> **BUILDING BACKGROUND** Trade and technology have turned the world into a "global village." People around the world wear clothes, eat foods, and use goods made in other countries. Global connections are bringing people around the world closer than ever before.

Globalization

In just seconds an e-mail message sent by a teenager in India beams all the way to a friend in London. A band in Seattle releases a song that becomes popular in China. People from New York to Singapore respond to a crisis in Brazil. These are all examples of **globalization**, the process in which countries are increasingly linked to each other through culture and trade.

What caused globalization? Improvements in transportation and communication over the past 100 years have brought the world closer together. Airplanes, telecommunications, and the Internet allow us to communicate and travel the world with ease. As a result, global culture and trade have increased.

Popular Culture

What might you have in common with a teenager in Japan? You probably have more in common than you think. You may use similar technology, wear similar clothes, and watch many of the same movies. You share the same global popular culture.

What You Will Learn...

Main Ideas

1. Globalization links the world's countries together through culture and trade.
2. The world community works together to solve global conflicts and crises.

The Big Idea

Fast, easy global connections have made cultural exchange, trade, and a cooperative world community possible.

Key Terms

globalization, *p. 97*
popular culture, *p. 98*
interdependence, *p. 99*
United Nations (UN), *p. 99*
humanitarian aid, *p. 100*

hmhsocialstudies.com
TAKING NOTES

Use the graphic organizer online to take notes on globalization and the world community.

More and more, people around the world are linked through popular culture. **Popular culture** refers to culture traits that are well known and widely accepted. Food, sports, music, and movies are all examples of our popular culture.

The United States has great influence on global popular culture. For example, American soft drinks are sold in almost every country in the world. Many popular American television shows are broadcast internationally. English has become the major global language. One-quarter of the world's people speak English. It has become the main language for international music, business, science, and education.

At the same time, the United States is influenced by global culture. Martial arts movies from Asia attract large audiences in the United States. Radio stations in the United States play music by African, Latin American, and European musicians. We even adopt many foreign words, like *sushi* and *plaza*, into English.

A Global Economy

The growth of the global economy has affected many businesses, especially the automobile industry. Automakers can now buy parts from countries all around the world, depending on where they can get the best price.

Many engines are man–ufactured in the United States and Canada.

Bumpers are often designed and produced in France, Germany, and the United States.

Tires come from a number of countries, including Mexico, South Korea, or Chile.

Global Trade

Globalization not only links the world's people, but it also connects businesses and affects trade. For centuries, societies have traded with each other. Improvements in transportation and communication have made global trade quicker and easier. For example, a shoe retailer in Chicago can order the sneakers she needs on a Web site from a company in China. The order can be flown to Chicago the next day and sold to customers that afternoon.

Many cars feature windows manufactured in Venezuela or the United States.

Seats are sometimes assembled in Japan from covers sewn in Mexico.

ANALYSIS SKILL **ANALYZING VISUALS**

From what different countries do automotive parts often originate?

The expansion of global trade has increased interdependence among the world's countries. **Interdependence** is a relationship between countries in which they rely on one another for resources, goods, or services. Many companies in one country often rely on goods and services produced in another country. For example, automakers in Europe might purchase auto parts made in the United States or Japan. Consumers also rely on goods produced elsewhere. For example, American shoppers buy bananas from Ecuador and tomatoes from Mexico. Global trade gives us access to goods from around the world.

READING CHECK **Finding Main Ideas** How has globalization affected the world?

A World Community

Some people call our world a global village. What do you think this means? Because of globalization, the world seems smaller. Places are more connected. What happens in one part of the world can affect the entire planet. Because of this, the world community works together to promote cooperation among countries in times of conflict and crisis.

The world community encourages cooperation by working to resolve global conflicts. From time to time, conflicts erupt among the countries of the world. Wars, trade disputes, and political disagreements can threaten the peace. Countries often join together to settle such conflicts. In 1945, for example, 51 nations created the United Nations. The **United Nations (UN)** is an organization of the world's countries that promotes peace and security around the globe.

The world community also promotes cooperation in times of crisis. A disaster may leave thousands of people in need.

FOCUS ON READING

What is the main idea of this paragraph? What facts are used to support that idea?

HISTORIC DOCUMENT
The Charter of the United Nations

Created in 1945, the United Nations is an organization of the world's countries that works to solve global problems. The Charter of the United Nations outlines the goals of the UN, some of which are included here.

We the Peoples of the United Nations Determined . . .

to save succeeding generations from the scourge [terror] of war . . .

to practice tolerance and live together in peace with one another as good neighbors, and

to unite our strength to maintain international peace and security, and

to ensure . . . that armed forces shall not be used, save [except] in the common interest, and

to employ international machinery [systems] for the promotion of the economic and social advancement of all peoples,

Have Resolved to Combine our Efforts to Accomplish these Aims.

—*from the Charter of the United Nations*

ANALYSIS SKILL **ANALYZING PRIMARY SOURCES**
What are some of the goals of the United Nations?

Earthquakes, floods, and drought can cause crises around the world. Groups from many nations often come together to provide **humanitarian aid**, or assistance to people in distress.

Organizations representing countries around the globe work to help in times of crisis. For example, in 2004 a tsunami, or huge tidal wave, devastated parts of Southeast Asia. Many organizations, like the United Nations Children's Fund (UNICEF) and the International Red Cross, stepped in to provide humanitarian aid to the victims of the tsunami. Some groups lend aid to refugees, or people who have been forced to flee their homes. Groups like Doctors Without Borders give medical aid to those in need around the world.

READING CHECK **Analyzing** How has globalization promoted cooperation?

SUMMARY In this section you learned how globalization links the countries of the world through shared culture and trade. Globalization allows organizations around the world to work together. They often solve conflicts and provide humanitarian aid.

Section 4 Assessment

hmhsocialstudies.com
ONLINE QUIZ

Reviewing Ideas, Terms, and Places

1. **a. Describe** What is **globalization**?
   b. Make Inferences How has **popular culture** influenced countries around the world?
   c. Evaluate In your opinion, has globalization hurt or helped the people of the world?
2. **a. Define** What is **humanitarian aid**?
   b. Draw Conclusions How has globalization promoted cooperation among countries?
   c. Predict What types of problems might lead to international cooperation?

Critical Thinking

3. **Identifying Cause and Effect** Use your notes and the graphic organizer at right to identify the effects that globalization has on our world.

Globalization → Effects / Effects / Effects

FOCUS ON WRITING

4. **Writing about Global Connections** What aspects of globalization could you include in your poster? Jot down your ideas in your notebook.

Chapter Review

Geography's Impact
video series
Review the video to answer the closing question:
Why do you think some peoples must work to preserve their cultures in the modern world?

Visual Summary

Use the visual summary below to help you review the main ideas of the chapter.

QUICK FACTS

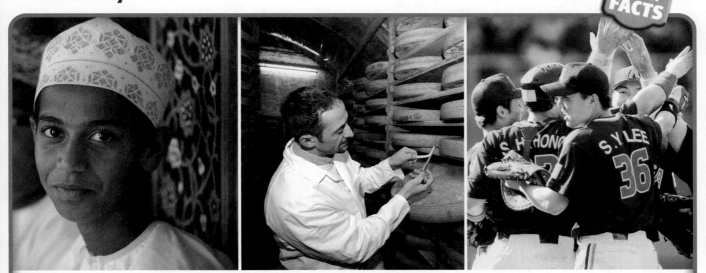

The world has many different cultures, or shared beliefs and practices.

The world's people practice different economic activities and systems.

Globalization brings people around the world closer than ever before.

Reviewing Vocabulary, Terms, and Places

Choose one word from each word pair to correctly complete each sentence below.

1. Members of a/an _____ often share the same religion, traditions, and language. **(ethnic group/population)**

2. People in a _____ are free to buy and sell goods as they please. **(command economy/ market economy)**

3. Organizations like the International Red Cross provide _____ to people in need around the world. **(humanitarian aid/cultural diffusion)**

4. _____, the process of moving from one place to live in another, is a cause of population change. **(Population density/Migration)**

5. A country with a strong economy and a high standard of living is considered a _____. **(developed country/developing country)**

Comprehension and Critical Thinking

SECTION 1 *(Pages 80–85)*

6. **a. Describe** What is cultural diversity?

   b. Analyze What causes cultures to change over time?

   c. Elaborate Describe some of the culture traits practiced by people in your community.

SECTION 2 *(Pages 86–90)*

7. **a. Describe** What does population density tell us about a place?

   b. Draw Conclusions Why do certain areas attract large populations?

   c. Elaborate Why do you think it is important for geographers to study population trends?

SECTION 3 *(Pages 91–95)*

8. **a. Recall** What is a command economy?

SECTION 3 *(continued)*

b. Make Inferences Why might developing countries have only primary and secondary economic activities?

c. Evaluate Do you think government is important in our everyday lives? Why or why not?

SECTION 4 *(Pages 97–100)*

9. a. Describe How have connections among the world's countries improved?

b. Analyze What impact has globalization had on world trade and culture?

c. Evaluate What do you think has been the most important result of globalization? Why?

Social Studies Skills

10. Organizing Information Practice organizing information by creating a graphic organizer for Section 3. Use the main ideas on the first page of the section for your large circles. Then write the subtopics under each main idea. Finally, identify supporting details for each subtopic.

Using the Internet

11. Activity: Writing a Report Population changes have a huge impact on the world around us. Countries around the world must deal with shrinking populations, growing populations, and other population issues. Through your online textbook, explore the issues surrounding global population. Then imagine you have been asked to report on global population trends to the United Nations. Write a report in which you identify world population trends and their impact on the world today.

Map Activity

Population Density *Use the map to the right to answer the questions that follow.*

12. What letter on the map indicates the least crowded area?

13. What letter on the map indicates the most densely crowded area?

14. Which letter indicates a region with 260–520 people per square mile (100–200 people per square km)?

FOCUS ON READING AND WRITING

Understanding Main Ideas *Read the paragraph in question 15 below. Then, write out the main idea of the paragraph.*

15. The ancient Greeks were the first to practice democracy. Since then many countries have adopted democratic government. The United Kingdom, South Korea, and Ghana all practice democracy. Democracy is the most widely used government in the world today.

16. Creating a Poster Review your notes about the world's cultures, populations, governments, and economies. Then, select a topic for your poster. On large sheet of paper, write a title that identifies your topic. Illustrate your poster with images that support your topic. Write a short caption explaining each image.

DIRECTIONS: *Read questions 1 through 7 and write the letter of the best response. Then read question 8 and write your own well-constructed response.*

1 **Which of the following is *most likely* a culture trait?**

A religion

B population density

C interdependence

D cultural diffusion

2 **What developments led to the rapid increase in world population in the last 200 years?**

A a decline in migration

B improvements in technology and communication

C a decrease in standard of living

D improvements in health care and agriculture

3 **Which economic system is used in the United States?**

A market economy

B command economy

C traditional economy

D domestic economy

4 **A government in which a single, powerful ruler exerts complete control is a**

A Communist state.

B democracy.

C dictatorship.

D republic.

5 **Global connections have improved as a result of**

A population growth.

B cultural diversity.

C the spread of democratic government.

D improvements in technology.

Developed and Developing Countries

Country	Per Capita GDP (U.S. $)	Life Expectancy at Birth	TVs per 1,000 People
Cameroon	$2,400	53.0	34
Singapore	$30,900	81.8	341
Ukraine	$7,600	67.9	433
Uruguay	$10,700	76.5	531

6 **Which of the countries in the chart above is *most likely* a developed country?**

A Cameroon

B Singapore

C Ukraine

D Uruguay

7 **Which of the following is an example of economic interdependence?**

A Cattle ranchers in Oklahoma sell beef to grocery stores in Maryland.

B Students in Germany use the Internet to communicate with scientists in Brazil.

C Construction companies in Canada build skyscrapers with steel imported from the United States.

D Immigrants from Russia settle in London.

8 **Extended Response** Using the data in the chart above, write a paragraph in which you compare and contrast the standard of living in Ukraine and Singapore.

Explaining a Process

21ST CENTURY

How does soil renewal work? How do cultures change? Often the first question we ask about something is how it works or what process it follows. One way we can answer these questions is by writing an explanation.

Assignment
Write a paper explaining one of these topics:
- how water recycles on Earth
- how agriculture developed

1. Prewrite
Choose a Process
- Choose one of the topics above to write about.
- Turn your topic into a big idea, or thesis. For example, your big idea might be "Water continually circulates from Earth's surface to the atmosphere and back."

> **TIP** **Organizing Information** Explanations should be in a logical order. You should arrange the steps in the process in chronological order, the order in which the steps take place.

Gather and Organize Information
- Look for information about your topic in your textbook, in the library, or on the Internet.
- Start a plan to organize support for your big idea. For example, look for the individual steps of the water cycle.

2. Write
Use a Writer's Framework

A Writer's Framework

Introduction
- Start with an interesting fact or question.
- Identify your big idea.

Body
- Create at least one paragraph for each point supporting the big idea. Add facts and details to explain each point.
- Use chronological order or order of importance.

Conclusion
- Summarize your main points in your final paragraph.

3. Evaluate and Revise
Review and Improve Your Paper
- Re-read your paper and make sure you have followed the framework.
- Make the changes needed to improve your paper.

Evaluation Questions for an Explanation of a Process
1. Do you begin with an interesting fact or question?
2. Does your introduction identify your big idea? Does it provide any background information your readers might need?
3. Do you have at least one paragraph for each point you are using to support the big idea?
4. Do you include facts and details to explain and illustrate each point?
5. Do you use chronological order or order of importance to organize your main points?

4. Proofread and Publish
Give Your Explanation the Finishing Touch
- Make sure you have capitalized the first word in every sentence.
- Check for punctuation at the end of every sentence.
- Think of a way to share your explanation.

5. Practice and Apply
Use the steps and strategies outlined in this workshop to write your explanation. Share your paper with others and find out whether the explanation makes sense to them.

References

Available @

↗ **hmhsocialstudies.com**

- Facts About the World
- Regions of the World Handbook
- Standardized Test-Taking Strategies
- Economics Handbook

Using Prior Knowledge

FOCUS ON READING

When you put together a puzzle, you search for pieces that are missing to complete the picture. As you read, you do the same thing when you use prior knowledge. You take what you already know about a subject and then add the information you are reading to create a full picture. The example below shows how using prior knowledge about computer mapping helped one reader fill in the pieces about how geographers use computer mapping.

In the past, maps were always drawn by hand. Many were not very accurate. Today, though, most maps are made using computers and satellite images. Through advances in mapmaking, we can make accurate maps on almost any scale, from the whole world to a single neighborhood, and keep them up to date.

From Section 3, The Branches of Geography

Computer Mapping	
What I know before reading	What else I learned
• My dad uses the computer to get a map for trips. • I can find maps on the Internet of states and countries.	• Maps have not always been very accurate. • Computers help make new kinds of maps that are more than just cities and roads. • These computer maps are an important part of geography.

YOU TRY IT!

Draw a chart like the one above. Think about what you know about satellite images and list this prior knowledge in the left column of your chart. Then read the passage below. Once you have read it, add what you learned about satellite images to the right column.

Much of the information gathered by these satellites is in the form of images. Geographers can study these images to see what an area looks like from above Earth. Satellites also collect information that we cannot see from the planet's surface. The information gathered by satellites helps geographers make accurate maps.

From Section 1, Studying Geography

Using Word Parts

FOCUS ON READING

Many English words are made up of several word parts: roots, prefixes, and suffixes. A root is the base of the word and carries the main meaning. A prefix is a letter or syllable added to the beginning of a root. A suffix is a letter or syllable added to the end to create new words. When you come across a new word, you can sometimes figure out the meaning by looking at its parts. Below are some common word parts and their meanings.

Common Roots		
Word Root	**Meaning**	**Sample Words**
-graph-	write, writing	autograph, biography
-vid-, -vis-	see	videotape, visible

Common Prefixes		
Prefix	**Meaning**	**Sample Words**
geo-	earth	geology
inter-	between, among	interpersonal, intercom
in-	not	ineffective
re-	again	restate, rebuild

Common Suffixes		
Suffix	**Meaning**	**Sample Words**
-ible	capable of	visible, responsible
-less	without	penniless, hopeless
-ment	result, action	commitment
-al	relating to	directional
-tion	the act or condition of	rotation, selection

YOU TRY IT!

Read the following words. First separate any prefixes or suffixes and identify the word's root. Use the chart above to define the root, the prefix, or the suffix. Then write a definition for each word.

geography	visualize	movement
seasonal	reshaping	interact
regardless	separation	invisible

Understanding Cause and Effect

FOCUS ON READING

Learning to identify causes and effects can help you understand geography. A **cause** is something that makes another thing happen. An **effect** is the result of something else that happened. A cause may have several effects, and an effect may have several causes. In addition, as you can see in the example below, causes and effects may occur in a chain. Then, each effect in turn becomes the cause for another event.

First cause

The Gulf Stream is a warm current that flows north along the U.S. East Coast. It then flows east across the Atlantic to become the North Atlantic Drift. As the warm current flows along northwestern Europe, it heats the air. Westerlies blow the warmed air across Europe. This process makes Europe warmer than it otherwise would be.

From Section 1, Weather and Climate

Last effect

Cause
Gulf Stream

Effect
Warm water flows along the coast of northwest Europe.

Effect
Warm water raises temperature of the air above.

Effect
Winds blow warm air across Europe.

Effect
Warm winds make Europe warmer.

YOU TRY IT!

Read the following sentences, and then use a graphic organizer like the one below right to analyze the cause and effects. Create as many boxes as you need to list the causes and effects.

Mountains also create wet and dry areas. . . A mountain forces wind blowing against it to rise. As it rises, the air cools and precipitation falls as rain or snow. Thus, the side of the mountain facing the wind is often green and lush. However, little moisture remains for the other side. This effect creates a rain shadow.

From Section 1, Weather and Climate

Cause → **Effect** → **Effect** → **Effect**

Understanding Main Ideas

FOCUS ON READING

Main ideas are like the hub of a wheel. The hub holds the wheel together, and everything circles around it. In a paragraph, the main idea holds the paragraph together and all the facts and details revolve around it. The main idea is usually stated clearly in a topic sentence, which may come at the beginning or end of a paragraph. Topic sentences always summarize the most important idea of a paragraph.

To find the main idea, ask yourself what one point is holding the paragraph together. See how the main idea in the following example holds all the details from the paragraph together.

A single country may also include more than one culture region within its borders. Mexico is one of many countries that is made up of different culture regions. People in northern Mexico and southern Mexico, for example, have different culture traits. The culture of northern Mexico tends to be more modern, while traditional culture remains strong in southern Mexico.

From Section 1, Culture

Mexico

A single country may also include more than one culture region within its borders.

Northern Mexico — modern culture

Southern Mexico — traditional culture

YOU TRY IT!

Read the following paragraph, and then use a graphic organizer like the one above to identify the main idea. Create as many circles as you need to list the supporting facts and details.

At the same time, the United States is influenced by global culture. Martial arts movies from Asia attract large audiences in the United States. Radio stations in the United States play music by African, Latin American, and European musicians. We even adopt many foreign words, like *sushi* and *plaza*, into English.

From Section 4, Global Connections

United States: Physical

Strait of Juan de Fuca

45°N

Mount Rainier
14,410 ft
(4,392 m)

Puget Sound

COAST RANGES

CASCADE RANGE

Columbia River

Willamette River

Franklin D. Roosevelt Lake

Pend Oreille Lake

Clark Fork

Flathead River

Flathead Lake

ROCKY

Milk River

Missouri River

Lake Sakakawea

Columbia Plateau

Bitterroot Range

Salmon River

Salmon River Mts.

Sawtooth Mts.

CONTINENTAL

Grand Tetons

Yellowstone Lake

Yellowstone River

Bighorn Mts.

Bighorn River

Powder River

Fort Peck Lake

Yellowstone River

Black Hills

Cheyenne River

White River

G R E A T

40°N

Cape Mendocino

Klamath River

Goose Lake

Shasta Lake

Pyramid Lake

Snake River

Great Salt Lake

Utah Lake

Wasatch Range

Gannett Peak
13,804 ft
(4,207 m)

Wind River Range

Wind River

Uinta Mts.

DIVIDE

Front Range

North Platte River

Niobrara River

Platte R

I N T E

125°W

San Francisco Bay

Sacramento River

Central Valley

SIERRA NEVADA

Lake Tahoe

GREAT

BASIN

Green River

Colorado River

Mount Elbert
14,433 ft
(4,400 m)

Pikes Peak
14,110 ft
(4,301 m)

South Platte River

Republican Riv

Smoky Hill Riv

P L

35°N

Monterey Bay

San Joaquin River

Coast Ranges

Mount Whitney
14,494 ft
(4,419 m)

Death Valley

Colorado River

Lake Mead

Grand Canyon

Lake Powell

San Juan River

COLORADO

PLATEAU

Sangre De Cristo Mts.

San Luis Valley

A I

PACIFIC
OCEAN

Channel Islands

Mojave Desert

Salton Sea

Imperial Valley

Painted Desert

DIVIDE

Rio Grande

Canadian River

N S

30°N

120°W

Gila River

Sonoran Desert

CONTINENTAL

Pecos River

Colo

Gulf of California

Amistad Reservoir

Rio Grande

MEXICO

To understand the relative locations of Alaska and Hawaii, as well as the vast distances separating them from the rest of the United States, see the world map.

Nueces

HAWAII

Kauai

Niihau

Oahu

Molokai

Maui

Lanai

Kahoolawe

PACIFIC OCEAN

22°N

Mauna Kea
13,796 ft
(4,206 m)

19°N

Hawaii

0   75   150 Miles
0   75   150 Kilometers
Projection: Mercator

ARCTIC OCEAN

BROOKS RANGE

RUSSIA

Arctic Circle

Bering Strait

Yukon River

Tanana River

ALASKA

RANGE

Mount McKinley
20,320 ft
(6,194 m)

CANADA

St. Lawrence Island

St. Matthew Island

Nunivak Island

Kuskokwim River

Bering Sea

55°N

50°N

Attu Island

PACIFIC OCEAN

ALEUTIAN ISLANDS

0   250   500 Miles
0   250   500 Kilometers
Projection: Albers Equal Area

Gulf of Alaska

Kodiak Island

Alexander Archipelago

55°N

CANADA

Isle
Royale
Mesabi Range
Lake Superior

Minnesota River
Mississippi River
Wisconsin River

Lake Michigan
Lake Huron
Lake Ontario
Lake Erie

St. Lawrence River
St. Lawrence Seaway
Lake Champlain
Adirondack Mts.
Catskill Mts.
ALLEGHENY PLATEAU
Susquehanna River
Hudson River
Green Mts.
White Mts.
Longfellow Mts.
Penobscot River
St. John River
Connecticut River
Cape Cod
Long Island Sound
Long Island

40°N

Des Moines River
Missouri River
Illinois River

Wabash River
Scioto River
Ohio River

Allegheny R.
Monongahela R.
Potomac River
Kanawha River
James River
Roanoke River
Delaware River
Delaware Bay
Chesapeake Bay

ATLANTIC
OCEAN

70°W

P L A I N S

Lake of the
Ozarks
OZARK PLATEAU

Keystone
Lake

Arkansas River
White River
Ouachita Mts.

Kansas R.

Lake Barkley
Cumberland River
Kentucky Lake
Tennessee River

APPALACHIAN MOUNTAINS
Cumberland Plateau
Great Smoky Mts.
BLUE RIDGE MOUNTAINS
PIEDMONT

Pamlico Sound
Cape Hatteras

35°N

ELEVATION
Feet   Meters
13,120   4,000
6,560   2,000
1,640   500
656   200
(Sea level) 0   0 (Sea level)
Below   Below
sea level sea level

0   100   200 Miles
0   100   200 Kilometers
Projection: Albers Equal Area

Saline River
Red River
Mississippi River
Pearl River
Tombigbee River
Alabama R.
Coosa River
Chattahoochee River
Oconee River
Savannah River
Altamaha River
Sea Islands

Toledo Bend Reservoir

G U L F   C O A S T A L   P L A I N

Chandeleur
Islands
Mississippi
Delta

N
W   E
S

Okefenokee
Swamp

Cape
Canaveral

FLORIDA PENINSULA

80°W

Gulf of Mexico

BAHAMAS

25°N

Lake Okeechobee

The Everglades
Cape Sable
Florida Keys

Straits of Florida

75°W

85°W
90°W
95°W

ATLAS

Strait of
Juan de Fuca

Puget
Sound

Franklin D.
Roosevelt Lake

Pend
Oreille

Seattle
Tacoma
Olympia
WASHINGTON

Spokane

45°N

Portland
Columbia River

Salem

Eugene

OREGON

Flathead
Lake

IDAHO

Boise

Sun Valley

Snake

River

Pocatello

Great Falls

Helena

MONTANA

Billings

Fort Peck
Lake

Missouri River

Yellowstone River

NORTH DAKO

Lake
Sakakawea

Bismarck

Yellowstone
Lake

WYOMING

Cheyenne

Lake
Oahe

SOUTH DAKOT

Pierre

Rapid City

NEBRASK

Cape
Mendocino

40°N

Goose
Lake

Shasta
Lake

Sacramento River

Pyramid
Lake

NEVADA

Reno
Carson City

ake Tahoe

Great
Salt
Lake

Ogden

Salt Lake City
Provo

Utah
Lake

UTAH

Green River

Platte R

Boulder
Vail
Aspen
Denver
Colorado
Springs

COLORADO

Pueblo

KANS

Arkansas River

35°N

Berkeley
Oakland
San Francisco
San Francisco Bay
San Jose

Sacramento

San Joaquin River

Monterey
Bay

Fresno

CALIFORNIA

Las
Vegas

Lake
Mead

Colorado River

Lake
Powell

Flagstaff

ARIZONA

Phoenix

Taos

Santa Fe

Albuquerque

NEW MEXICO

OKLAHO

Canadian River

Amarillo

Oklahom

La

125°W

Santa Barbara
Ventura
Los
Angeles
Long
Beach
Anaheim
Santa Ana
San Diego

Channel

Islands

Riverside
Palm Springs

Salton
Sea

PACIFIC

OCEAN

30°N

120°W

Gulf of
California

Gila

Casa Grande

River

Tucson

Las Cruces

El Paso

Lubbock

Abilene

Midland
Odessa

Brazos River

Fort W

TEXA

Pecos River

Colorado

Rio

Amistad
Reservoir

Aus

To understand the relative locations of Alaska and
Hawaii, as well as the vast distances separating them
from the rest of the United States, see the world map.

San Antonio

Grande

Corpus Chr

Laredo

MEXICO

Kauai

Niihau

Oahu

HAWAII

Honolulu

PACIFIC
OCEAN

Molokai

Lanai

Maui

Kahoolawe

22°N

155°W

N

W   E

S

Hilo

Hawaii

19°N

0   75   150 Miles

0   75   150 Kilometers

Projection: Mercator

160°W

ARCTIC OCEAN

Arctic Circle

RUSSIA

Bering

Strait

Nome

Yukon River

St. Lawrence
Island

St. Matthew
Island

Nunivak
Island

Fairbanks

CANADA

ALASKA

Anchorage
Valdez

Skagway

Juneau

Gulf of Alaska

Kodiak Island

Alexander
Archipelago

55°N

170°E

Bering Sea

50°N

Attu Island

N

W   E

S

0   250   500 Miles

0   250   500 Kilometers

Projection: Albers Equal Area

ALEUTIAN
ISLANDS

180°

170°W

160°W

150°W

140°W

55°N

PACIFIC
OCEAN

CANADA

MINNESOTA

Duluth
Superior
Marquette
Sault Ste. Marie
Lake Superior

MICHIGAN

MAINE

Augusta

WISCONSIN

Green Bay

Minneapolis
St. Paul
Madison
Milwaukee

Grand Rapids
Lansing
Saginaw
Detroit
Ann Arbor

Lake Michigan
Lake Huron

Burlington
Montpelier
Portland

Lake Champlain
VT
NH
Concord
Manchester

St. Lawrence River

Lake Ontario
Rochester
Syracuse
Albany
Springfield
MA
Boston
Worcester
Providence
Cape Cod

IOWA

Cedar Rapids
Davenport
Des Moines

Rockford
Chicago
Gary
South Bend
Fort Wayne

Toledo
Cleveland
Youngstown
Akron

Buffalo
NEW YORK

Hartford
CT
RI
New Haven
Bridgeport
Long Island Sound
Yonkers
Long Island
Newark
New York City

Hudson R.
Connecticut R.
Lake Erie
Erie

Peoria

Springfield

OHIO

Columbus

PENNSYLVANIA
Allentown
Harrisburg
Pittsburgh

Susquehanna River

Jersey City
Trenton
NJ
Camden
Philadelphia
Atlantic City

MISSOURI

Kansas City
Kansas City

ILLINOIS

St. Louis
East St. Louis
Jefferson City

INDIANA
Indianapolis
Dayton
Cincinnati

Illinois River

Baltimore
MD
Annapolis
DE
Dover

Delaware Bay

Washington, D.C.

Lake of the Ozarks

Louisville
Evansville
Frankfort
Lexington

WEST VIRGINIA
Charleston

VIRGINIA
Richmond
Newport News
Norfolk
Virginia Beach

Chesapeake Bay

ATLANTIC OCEAN

40°N

70°W

Keystone Lake
Tulsa

Springfield

Ohio River
KENTUCKY
Lake Barkley

Cape Hatteras

35°N

Fayetteville

Nashville
Knoxville
Asheville

Greensboro
Durham
Winston-Salem
Raleigh
Charlotte

Kentucky Lake
Kentucky River

ARKANSAS
Little Rock
Pine Bluff

Memphis
TENNESSEE
Chattanooga
Huntsville

NORTH CAROLINA

Greenville
SOUTH CAROLINA
Columbia

Savannah River

National capital
State capitals
Other cities

0   100   200 Miles
0   100   200 Kilometers

Projection: Albers Equal Area

Shreveport

MISSISSIPPI
Vicksburg
Jackson
Meridian
Montgomery

Mississippi River

ALABAMA
Birmingham
Columbus
Atlanta
Macon

GEORGIA

Charleston

Sea Islands

Savannah

30°N

Toledo Bend Reservoir

LOUISIANA
Baton Rouge
Biloxi
New Orleans

Red River

Mobile
Pensacola
Tallahassee
Jacksonville

Chattahoochee R.

Beaumont
Houston
Galveston

Chandeleur Islands

Gainesville

FLORIDA
Orlando
Tampa
St. Petersburg

Cape Canaveral

80°W

BAHAMAS

25°N

75°W

Gulf of Mexico

N
W   E
S

Fort Myers
Fort Lauderdale
Miami

Lake Okeechobee

Cape Sable
Florida Keys
Straits of Florida

95°W
90°W
85°W

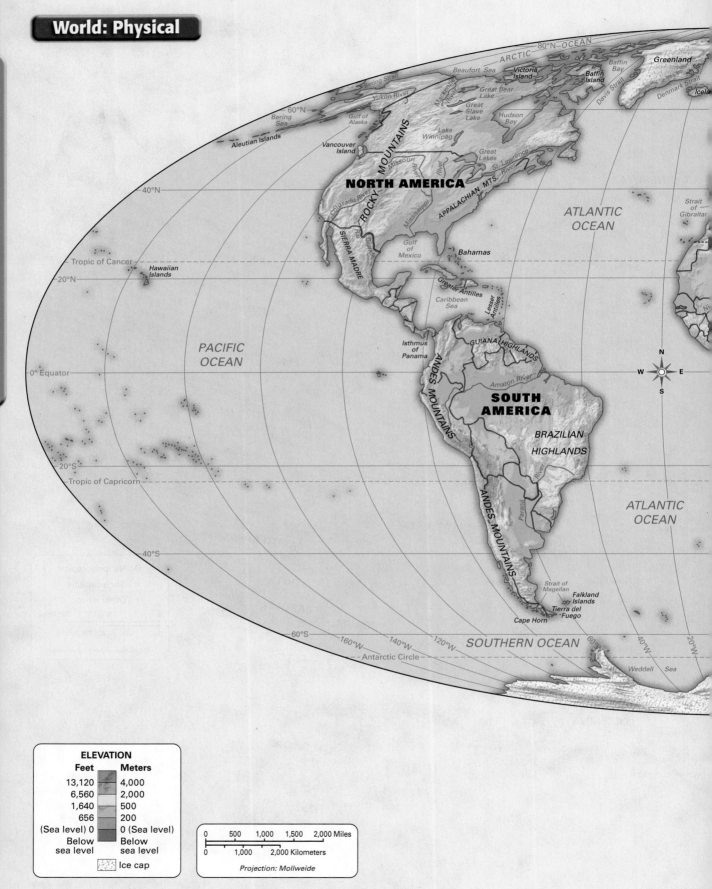

ARCTIC OCEAN
80°N

Beaufort Sea
Victoria Island
Baffin Island
Baffin Bay
Greenland
Davis Strait
Denmark Strait
Iceland

Bering Strait
Yukon River
Great Bear Lake
60°N
Bering Sea
Great Slave Lake
Hudson Bay

Aleutian Islands
Gulf of Alaska
Lake Winnipeg
Great Lakes
St. Lawrence River

Vancouver Island
ROCKY MOUNTAINS
Missouri River

NORTH AMERICA
40°N
Colorado River
Mississippi
APPALACHIAN MTS.
ATLANTIC OCEAN
Strait of Gibraltar

SIERRA MADRE
Rio Grande
Gulf of Mexico
Bahamas

Tropic of Cancer
Hawaiian Islands
20°N
Greater Antilles
Caribbean Sea
Lesser Antilles

PACIFIC OCEAN
Isthmus of Panama
GUIANA HIGHLANDS

0° Equator
ANDES MOUNTAINS
Amazon River
N
W   E
S

SOUTH AMERICA
BRAZILIAN HIGHLANDS

20°S
Tropic of Capricorn
Paraná River
ATLANTIC OCEAN

ANDES MOUNTAINS
40°S

Strait of Magellan
Falkland Islands
Tierra del Fuego
Cape Horn

60°S
160°W   140°W   120°W
SOUTHERN OCEAN
60°W   40°W   20°W
Antarctic Circle
Weddell Sea

ELEVATION

Feet		Meters
13,120		4,000
6,560		2,000
1,640		500
656		200
(Sea level) 0		0 (Sea level)
Below sea level		Below sea level

Ice cap

0   500   1,000   1,500   2,000 Miles
0   1,000   2,000 Kilometers

Projection: Mollweide

ARCTIC 80°N OCEAN

North Cape
Barents Sea
Kara Sea
Laptev Sea
East Siberian Sea

EUROPE

Ural Mountains

Ob River
Yenisei River
Lena River
Kolyma River

Baltic Sea

Volga River

Caspian Sea

Black Sea

60°N

Sea of Okhotsk

KAMCHATKA PENINSULA

Mediterranean Sea

ASIA

GOBI

Balqash Lake
Aral Sea

ALTAY

Lake Baikal

Amur River

Sakhalin Island

40°N

Hokkaido

Honshu

ARABIAN PENINSULA

Tigris River
Euphrates River
Persian Gulf

AFRICA

HIMALAYAS

Thar Desert

Ganges River

Huang He (Yellow River)

Chang Jiang (Yangzi River)

Mekong River

East China Sea

Shikoku
Kyushu

Taiwan

Tropic of Cancer
20°N

Arabian Sea

Bay of Bengal

South China Sea

Philippine Islands

PACIFIC OCEAN

Sri Lanka

Strait of Malacca

Congo River

Lake Tanganyika
Lake Victoria

MALAY PENINSULA

Borneo

Celebes

New Guinea

Solomon Islands

0° Equator

Sumatra

Java

INDIAN OCEAN

Coral Sea

New Hebrides

Fiji Islands

Madagascar

GREAT SANDY DESERT

AUSTRALIA

GREAT DIVIDING RANGE

New Caledonia

20°S

KALAHARI DESERT

Mozambique Channel

GREAT VICTORIA DESERT

Darling River

Tropic of Capricorn

Cape of Good Hope

Tasman Sea

North Island

NEW ZEALAND

Tasmania

South Island

20°E
40°E

SOUTHERN OCEAN

120°E

140°E

160°E

60°S

ANTARCTICA

ATLAS

Denmark Strait

Iceland

North Cape

Barents Sea

Kara Sea

60°N

KJØLEN MTS.

N
W E
S

North Sea

Baltic Sea

URAL MTS.

Volga River

0   250   500 Miles
0   250   500 Kilometers

Projection: Mollweide

50°N

British Isles

NORTHERN EUROPEAN PLAIN

ATLANTIC OCEAN

Bay of Biscay

Danube

ALPS

Black Sea

40°N

IBERIAN PENINSULA

Mediterranean Sea

Crete

Strait of Gibraltar

World: Political

ARCTIC OCEAN

Greenland
(DENMARK)

ALASKA
(U.S.)

Godthåb

ICE

60°N

CANADA

Aleutian Islands

Vancouver   Winnipeg

Ottawa   Montreal

NORTH
AMERICA

Chicago   Toronto

UNITED
STATES

New York City

ATLANTIC
OCEAN

40°N

Washington,
D.C.

Casabla

MORO

Los Angeles

Houston

Bermuda
(U.K.)

Western
Sahara
(Claimed by
Morocco)

MEXICO

Tropic of Cancer

Mexico
City

20°N

HAWAII
(U.S.)

MAURITA

Nouakchott

CAPE VERDE   SENEGAL
Dakar

Caracas

GAMBIA
GUINEA-BISSAU   GUINE

VENEZUELA   GUYANA

Bogotá

Georgetown   SURINAME

SIERRA
LEONE

PACIFIC
OCEAN

Paramaribo   French Guiana
(FRANCE)

LIBER

COLOMBIA

Quito

0° Equator

ECUADOR

KIRIBATI

Galápagos
Islands
(ECUADOR)

N

PERU

W   E

SOUTH
AMERICA

S

SAMOA

American
Samoa

BRAZIL

Lima

Brasília

BOLIVIA

20°S

TONGA

La Paz

Sucre

Tropic of Capricorn

Rio de Janeiro

PARAGUAY

São Paulo

CHILE

Asunción

ATLANTIC
OCEAN

URUGUAY

Santiago

40°S

Buenos
Aires

Montevideo

ARGENTINA

⊛ National capital

● Other city

Falkland
Islands
(U.K.)

0   500   1,000 Miles

0   500 1,000 Kilometers

South
Georgia
(U.K.)

South San
Islands

Projection: Mollweide

60°S

160°W

140°W

120°W

SOUTHERN OCEAN

60°

40°

20°

Antarctic Circle

90°W   80°W

70°W

FLORIDA
(U.S.)

Tropic of Cancer

0   200   400 Miles

Nassau

60°W

0   200   400 Kilometers

BAHAMAS

Projection: Mercator

Havana

Turks and Caicos Is.
(U.K.)

ATLANTIC   OCEAN

20°N

Gulf of
Mexico

CUBA

Cayman Is.
(U.K.)

HAITI   DOMINICAN
REPUBLIC

Virgin Islands
(U.S. and U.K.)

1

MEXICO

BELIZE

Port-au-Prince

Santo

Puerto Rico

2

Guadeloupe (FRANCE)

Belmopan

JAMAICA

Kingston

Domingo

(U.S.)

3

GUATEMALA

HONDURAS

Caribbean   Sea

Netherlands

4

Martinique (FRANCE)

Guatemala City

Tegucigalpa

Antilles
(NETHERLANDS)

5   6

San Salvador

NICARAGUA

Aruba
(NETHERLANDS)

7

EL SALVADOR

Managua

Port-of-
Spain

TRINIDAD AND
TOBAGO

N

COSTA RICA

Panama

W   E

City

10°N

S

San José

PANAMA

PACIFIC   OCEAN

COLOMBIA

VENEZUELA

GUYANA

COUNTRY	CAPITAL
1 Antigua and Barbuda	St. Johns
2 St. Kitts and Nevis	Basseterre
3 Dominica	Roseau
4 St. Lucia	Castries
5 St. Vincent and the Grenadines	Kingstown
6 Barbados	Bridgetown
7 Grenada	St. George's

ATLAS

	COUNTRY	CAPITAL
1	Czech Republic	Prague
2	Slovakia	Bratislava
3	Slovenia	Ljubljana
4	Croatia	Zagreb
5	Bosnia and Herzegovina	Sarajevo
6	Macedonia	Skopje
7	Serbia	Belgrade
8	Montenegro	Podgorica
9	Lithuania	Vilnius
10	Latvia	Riga
11	Estonia	Tallinn
12	Kosovo	Pristina

North America: Physical

ASIA

ARCTIC OCEAN

EUROPE

+North Pole

POLAR ICE PACK

Queen
Elizabeth
Islands

Ellesmere Island

Greenland

Baffin
Bay

St. Lawrence
Island

Nunivak
Island

Bering
Sea

Bering Strait

BROOKS RANGE

Yukon River

Beaufort
Sea

Banks
Island

Victoria
Island

Baffin Island

Davis Strait

Denmark Strait

Arctic Circle

Cape
Farewell

ALASKA RANGE

Mt. McKinley
20,320 ft
(6,194 m)

YUKON
PLATEAU

Great
Bear
Lake

Mackenzie
River

Southampton
Island

Hudson Strait

Labrador
Sea

Kodiak
Island

Gulf of
Alaska

Alexander
Archipelago

Queen
Charlotte
Islands

Vancouver
Island

ROCKY

Peace River

Great
Slave
Lake

Lake
Athabasca

Coats
Island

Mansel
Island

Hudson
Bay

CANADIAN

SHIELD

Anticosti
Island

Newfoundland

PACIFIC
OCEAN

Mount Rainier
14,410 ft
(4,392 m)

CASCADE RANGE

Columbia River

Fraser River

Athabasca
River

Saskatchewan
River

Nelson River

Lake
Winnipeg

Prince
Edward
Island

Gulf of
St. Lawrence

St. Lawrence River

Cape
Breton
Island

Snake River

MOUNTAINS

Missouri River

Lake
Superior

Lake
Michigan

Lake
Huron

Lake
Ontario

APPALACHIAN MOUNTAINS

Cape Cod

Long
Island

ATLANTIC
OCEAN

SIERRA NEVADA

CENTRAL RANGES

GREAT
BASIN

Great
Salt
Lake

BLACK
HILLS

Lake
Erie

GREAT

PLAINS

Platte
River

INTERIOR PLAINS

Mississippi River

Ohio River

Cumberland R.

PIEDMONT

Cape
Hatteras

Bermuda

DEATH
VALLEY

Mount Whitney
14,494 ft
(4,419 m)

COLORADO
PLATEAU

Colorado River

OZARK
PLATEAU

Arkansas River

Tennessee
River

ATLANTIC COASTAL PLAIN

Cape
Mendocino

COAST RANGES

Gila River

Red River

Brazos River

Mississippi River

Cape
Canaveral

Tropic of Cancer

Guadalupe
Island

BAJA CALIFORNIA

Rio Grande

GULF COASTAL PLAIN

FLORIDA
PENINSULA

Florida
Keys

Bahamas

SIERRA MADRE
OCCIDENTAL

SIERRA MADRE
ORIENTAL

Gulf of
Mexico

Straits of
Florida

Cuba

Greater Antilles

Hispaniola

Puerto
Rico

Lesser
Antilles

Popocatépetl
17,887 ft (5,452 m)

YUCATÁN
PENINSULA

Jamaica

Caribbean Sea

Trinidad

SIERRA MADRE DEL SUR

CENTRAL
AMERICA

Lake
Nicaragua

ISTHMUS OF
PANAMA

SOUTH
AMERICA

0° Equator

ELEVATION

Feet	Meters
13,120	4,000
6,560	2,000
1,640	500
656	200
(Sea level) 0	0 (Sea level)
Below sea level	Below sea level

Ice cap

0   300   600 Miles

0   300   600 Kilometers

Projection: Azimuthal Equal Area

North America: Political

ASIA

ARCTIC OCEAN
+ North Pole

EUROPE

ICELAND

St. Lawrence Island
Bering Sea
Nunivak Island
Point Barrow

ALASKA (U.S.)
Anchorage
Kodiak Island
Alexander Archipelago
Juneau
Queen Charlotte Islands
Vancouver Island

Queen Elizabeth Islands
Ellesmere Island
Greenland (DENMARK)
Banks Island
Beaufort Sea
Baffin Bay
Victoria Island
Baffin Island
Davis Strait
Cape Farewell
Denmark Strait

Great Bear Lake
Great Slave Lake

Southampton Island
Coats Island
Mansel Island
Hudson Strait
Hudson Bay

Labrador Sea
Arctic Circle

PACIFIC OCEAN

Edmonton
Calgary
Vancouver
Seattle
Portland

CANADA
Lake Winnipeg
Winnipeg

Lake Superior

Anticosti Island
Newfoundland
St. Pierre and Miquelon (FRANCE)
Prince Edward Island
Gulf of St. Lawrence
Cape Breton Island
Quebec
Montreal

Minneapolis
Milwaukee
Chicago
Lake Michigan
Lake Huron
Detroit
Cleveland
Columbus
Ottawa
Toronto
Lake Ontario
Lake Erie

Boston
Cape Cod
New York City
Philadelphia
Baltimore
Washington, D.C.

ATLANTIC OCEAN

San Francisco
San Jose
Los Angeles
San Diego
Tijuana

Great Salt Lake
Salt Lake City
Denver
Kansas City

UNITED STATES
Memphis
Phoenix
Dallas
Austin
San Antonio
Houston

Indianapolis
St. Louis

Norfolk

Birmingham
Atlanta

Jacksonville

Bermuda (U.K.)

Gulf of California
Monterrey

MEXICO
Guadalajara
Mexico City
Puebla
Mérida

New Orleans
Gulf of Mexico
Florida Keys

Tropic of Cancer

Miami
Nassau
BAHAMAS
Havana
Straits of Florida
CUBA

Turks and Caicos Islands (U.K.)

Cayman Is. (U.K.)
Kingston
JAMAICA
HAITI
Port-au-Prince
Santo Domingo
DOMINICAN REPUBLIC
Puerto Rico (U.S.)
San Juan
Virgin Is. (U.S., U.K.)
Martinique (FRANCE)

ST. KITTS & NEVIS
ANTIGUA & BARBUDA
Guadeloupe (FRANCE)
DOMINICA
BARBADOS
ST. LUCIA
ST. VINCENT AND THE GRENADINES
GRENADA

Belmopan
BELIZE
GUATEMALA
Guatemala City
San Salvador
EL SALVADOR
HONDURAS
Tegucigalpa
NICARAGUA
Managua
San José
COSTA RICA
Caribbean Sea
Panama Canal
Panama City
PANAMA
Aruba (NETHERLANDS)
Netherlands Antilles (NETHERLANDS)
TRINIDAD AND TOBAGO

SOUTH AMERICA

Equator

Legend:
- ⊛ National capital
- • Other city

0 300 600 Miles
0 300 600 Kilometers

Projection: Azimuthal Equal-Area

South America: Physical

CENTRAL AMERICA

Caribbean Sea

Panama Canal

Gulf of Panama

Malpelo Island

Margarita Island

Tobago

Trinidad

Orinoco River Delta

Lake Maracaibo

LLANOS

Orinoco River

Cauca River

Meta River

Angel Falls

GUIANA

HIGHLANDS

Devil's Island
Cape Orange

Mount Tolima
18,425 ft
(5,616 m)

Magdalena River

Orinoco River

Amazon River Delta

ATLANTIC OCEAN

Caquetá River

Rio Negro

Amazon River

Japurá River

AMAZON

Mount Chimborazo
20,561 ft
(6,267 m)

Marañón River

Amazon River

BASIN

Tapajós River

Galápagos Islands

0° Equator

Gulf of Guayaquil

Juruá River

Amazon River

Ucayali River

Purus River

Madeira River

Xingu River

Tocantins River

Tocantins River

Parnaíba River

0° Equator

Mount Huascarán
22,205 ft
(6,768 m)

ANDES

River

Beni River

Mamoré River

MATO GROSSO
PLATEAU

BRAZILIAN

Araguaia River

São Francisco River

HIGHLANDS

10°S

PACIFIC OCEAN

Lake Titicaca

Ancohuma Peak
20,958 ft
(6,388 m)

River

Pilcomayo River

Lake Poopó

ATACAMA DESERT

CHACO

Paraguay River

BRAZILIAN
PLATEAU

20°S

San Ambrosio Island

Tropic of Capricorn

ANDES

Salado River

Paraná River

Uruguay River

Tropic of Capricorn

San Félix Island

Juan Fernández Islands

Mount Aconcagua
22,834 ft
(6,960 m)

Salado River

Paraná River

Rio de la Plata

ATLANTIC OCEAN

30°S

30°S

ELEVATION

PAMPAS

Colorado River

Gulf of San Matías

Feet		Meters
13,120		4,000
6,560		2,000
1,640		500
656		200
(Sea level) 0		0 (Sea level)
Below sea level		Below sea level

Chiloé Island

Chonos Archipelago

PATAGONIA

Gulf of San Jorge

Cape Tres Puntas

0   250   500 Miles
0   250   500 Kilometers

Projection: Azimuthal Equal Area

Bahía Grande

Strait of Magellan

Falkland Islands

Tierra del Fuego

South Georgia Islands

Cape Horn

South America: Political

CENTRAL
AMERICA

Caribbean Sea

Barranquilla
Cartagena
Caracas
Lake
Maracaibo
VENEZUELA
ATLANTIC
OCEAN

Medellín
Bogotá
COLOMBIA
Georgetown
Paramaribo
GUYANA
Cayenne
SURINAME
French
Guiana
(FRANCE)

Malpelo
Island
(COLOMBIA)
Cali

Quito
ECUADOR
Guayaquil

Galápagos
Islands
(ECUADOR)

Belém

PERU

BRAZIL

Recife

Trujillo

Callao
Lima

PACIFIC
OCEAN
Lake
Titicaca
La Paz
Lake
Poopó
BOLIVIA
Sucre

Brasília

Salvador

Arequipa

Belo Horizonte

PARAGUAY

Campinas
São Paulo
Rio de Janeiro
Tropic of
Capricorn

Asunción
Curitiba

Tropic of Capricorn

San Ambrosio
Island
(CHILE)
San Félix Island
(CHILE)

CHILE

Pôrto Alegre

Córdoba
Juan Fernández
Islands
(CHILE)
Valparaíso
Santiago
Rosario
Buenos Aires
URUGUAY
Montevideo

ATLANTIC
OCEAN

ARGENTINA

• National capital
• Other city

0   250   500 Miles
0   250   500 Kilometers

Projection: Azimuthal Equal-Area

Strait of
Magellan
Falkland
Islands (U.K.)

Tierra del
Fuego

South Georgia
Island
(U.K.)

ATLAS

ASIA

SOUTHWEST
ASIA

URAL MOUNTAINS

Pachora River

Barents Sea

North Cape

KOLA
PENINSULA

White
Sea

North Dvina River

Lake
Onega

Lake
Ladoga

Rybinsk
Reservoir

Kama River

Volga River

Ob River

Ural River

Caspian Sea

Mt. Elbrus
18,510 ft (5,642 m)

CAUCASUS MTS.

Don River

Sea of
Azov

CRIMEAN
PENINSULA

Black Sea

NORTHERN EUROPEAN PLAIN

Dnipro River

Volga River

Dniester River

Nistru River

TRANSYLVANIAN
ALPS

CARPATHIAN

Danube River

BALKAN
PENINSULA

Sea of
Marmara

Aegean
Sea

Rhodes

Crete

CENTRAL RUSSIAN PLAINS

Gulf of Finland

Daugava R.

Baltic Sea

Vistula River

Oder River

Elbe River

Rhine River

Danube River

Po River

ALPS

DINARIC ALPS

Adriatic Sea

APENNINES

Tiber River

Tyrrhenian Sea

Sicily

Malta

Mediterranean Sea

ARCTIC OCEAN

KJOLEN MOUNTAINS

Lake
Vänern

Lake
Vättern

Kattegat

Skagerrak

Lake
Mälaren

Gulf of Bothnia

North
Sea

English Channel

Seine River

Loire River

Garonne River

Bay of
Biscay

Rhône River

Lake
Geneva

Mont Blanc
15,781 ft (4,810 m)

PYRENEES

Corsica

Sardinia

Balearic Islands

Iceland

Norwegian
Sea

Faeroe
Islands

Shetland
Islands

Orkney
Islands

Hebrides

British
Isles

Irish Sea

PENNINES

Thames
River

Cape Finisterre

IBERIAN
PENINSULA

Duero River

Tagus River

Guadiana River

Guadalquivir River

Ebro River

Strait of
Gibraltar

ATLANTIC
OCEAN

AFRICA

Arctic Circle

N · E · S · W

Projection: Azimuthal Equal Area

Europe: Physical

ELEVATION

Feet	Meters
13,120	4,000
6,560	2,000
1,640	500
656	200
(Sea level) 0	0 (Sea level)
Below
sea level	Below
sea level

Ice cap

300 Miles
150

300 Kilometers
150

0

Europe: Political

- ✪ National capital
- • Other city

	300 Miles
0	150	300 Kilometers
0	150	

Projection: Azimuthal Equal-Area

ASIA

URAL MOUNTAINS

RUSSIA

Nizhny Novgorod

Moscow

FINLAND

St. Petersburg

Tallinn
ESTONIA

Riga
LATVIA

Helsinki

LITHUANIA
Vilnius

RUSSIA

Minsk
BELARUS

Kiev
UKRAINE

MOLDOVA
Chișinău

Bucharest
ROMANIA

Sofia
BULGARIA

SOUTHWEST ASIA

Black Sea

Caspian Sea

Barents Sea

White Sea

North Cape

ARCTIC OCEAN

Gulf of Bothnia

SWEDEN

Stockholm

Göteborg

Baltic Sea

Warsaw
POLAND

Kraków

Berlin
GERMANY

Dresden

Prague
CZECH REPUBLIC

SLOVAKIA
Bratislava

Budapest
HUNGARY

Vienna
AUSTRIA

SLOVENIA
Ljubljana

CROATIA
Zagreb

BOSNIA AND
HERZEGOVINA
Sarajevo

Belgrade
SERBIA

MONTENEGRO
Podgorica

KOSOVO
Pristina

Skopje
MACEDONIA

Tirana
ALBANIA

GREECE
Athens

Rhodes

Crete

Aegean Sea

Sea

NORWAY

Oslo

Bergen

DENMARK
Copenhagen

Hamburg

North Sea

THE NETHERLANDS
Amsterdam

Cologne
Bonn

BELGIUM
Brussels

LUXEMBOURG
Luxembourg

SWITZERLAND
Bern

LIECHTENSTEIN
Vaidiz

Munich

Milan

Lake Geneva

MONACO
Monaco

SAN MARINO
San Marino

VATICAN CITY
Rome
ITALY

Naples

Sicily

MALTA
Valletta

Mediterranean Sea

ICELAND
Reykjavik

Arctic Circle

Faeroe Islands
(DENMARK)

Shetland Islands

SCOTLAND
Edinburgh

Belfast
NORTHERN IRELAND

IRELAND
Dublin

Liverpool

ENGLAND
London

WALES

UNITED KINGDOM

British Isles

English Channel

Channel Islands
(U.K.)

Paris
FRANCE

Lyon

Marseille

Corsica
(FRANCE)

Sardinia
(ITALY)

PYRENEES

ANDORRA
Andorra la Vella

Barcelona

Balearic Islands
(SPAIN)

Bay of Biscay

ATLANTIC OCEAN

SPAIN
Madrid

Valencia

Seville

Gibraltar
(U.K.)

Strait of Gibraltar

AFRICA

PORTUGAL
Lisbon

Asia: Physical

ELEVATION

Feet	Meters
13,120	4,000
6,560	2,000
1,640	500
656	200
0 (Sea level)	0 (Sea level)
Below sea level	Below sea level

Ice cap

0   250   500   750 Miles
0   250   500   750 Kilometers

Projection: Two-Point Equidistant

AUSTRALIA

PACIFIC OCEAN

Equator

Maoke Mountains

New Guinea

Arafura Sea

Banda Sea

Moluccas

Celebes Sea

Celebes

Moluccas

Java Sea

Bangka

Java

Sumatra

Mentawai Islands

Borneo

South China Sea

Hainan

Philippines

Mindanao

Luzon

Luzon Strait

Taiwan

East China Sea

Ryukyu Islands

Okinawa

Korea Strait

Kyushu

Shikoku

Honshu

Hokkaido

Sea of Japan (East Sea)

Kuril Islands

Sakhalin Island

Sea of Okhotsk

KAMCHATKA PENINSULA

CENTRAL RANGE

Bering Sea

Aleutian Islands

Wrangel Island

New Siberian Islands

KOLYMA MTS.

CHERSKIY RANGE

VERKHOYANSKY RANGE

Lena River

Aldan River

STANOVOY MOUNTAINS

YABLONOVY RANGE

Shilka River

Amur River

GREATER KHINGAN RANGE

NORTH CHINA PLAIN

Yellow Sea

Yellow River

Huang He

QIN LING

Xi River

Gulf of Tonkin

Hong River

BOHAI HILLS

MONGOLIAN PLATEAU

G O B I

Chang Jiang (Yangtze River)

INDOCHINA PENINSULA

Mekong River

Chao Phraya River

Gulf of Thailand

MALAY PENINSULA

Andaman Sea

Nicobar Islands

Andaman Islands

S I B E R I A

CENTRAL SIBERIAN PLATEAU

TAYMYR PENINSULA

North Land

North Pole

Severnaya River

Tunguska River

Angara River

Lower Tunguska River

Lake Baikal

SAYAN MOUNTAINS

ALTAY MOUNTAINS

TIAN SHAN

TARIM BASIN

TAKLIMAKAN DESERT

KUNLUN MOUNTAINS

PLATEAU OF TIBET

Nu River

Mount Everest 29,035 ft (8,850 m)

H I M A L A Y A S

Brahmaputra River

INDO-GANGETIC PLAIN

Ganges River

DECCAN PLATEAU

Godavari River

EASTERN GHATS

WESTERN GHATS

Bay of Bengal

Sri Lanka

Maldives

Lakshadweep Islands

INDIAN OCEAN

WEST SIBERIAN PLAIN

Ob River

Yenisey River

Irtysh River

Ishim River

Tobol River

URAL MOUNTAINS

Ural River

KAZAKH UPLANDS

Balqash Lake

Syr Darya

Aral Sea

TURAN LOWLAND

KYZYL KUM

Amu Darya

KARA KUM

HINDU KUSH

Indus River

Sutlej River

THAR DESERT

GREAT SALT DESERT

USTYURT PLATEAU

Caspian Sea

CAUCASUS MTS.

Mount Ararat 16,945 ft (5,165 m)

ANATOLIAN PLATEAU

ZAGROS MTS.

Tigris River

Euphrates River

Persian Gulf

Gulf of Oman

Arabian Sea

Socotra Island

Gulf of Aden

RUB' AL-KHALI

AN-NAFUD

SYRIAN DESERT

SINAI PENINSULA

Red Sea

Cyprus

Mediterranean Sea

EUROPE

Black Sea

Bosporus

Franz Josef Land

Novaya Zemlya

Kara Sea

Barents Sea

Arctic Circle

AFRICA

Tropic of Cancer

Asia: Political

National capitals
Other cities

0 250 500 750 Miles
0 250 500 750 Kilometers
Projection: Two-Point Equidistant

EUROPE

PACIFIC
OCEAN

AUSTRALIA

New Guinea

Arafura Sea

TIMOR-LESTE

Dili

Aleutian Islands

Bering Sea

Sea of Okhotsk

Kuril Islands (RUSSIA)

Sakhalin Island

Yokohama
Tokyo
Sapporo
JAPAN
Vladivostok
Osaka
Kyoto
Hiroshima
Nagasaki
Ryukyu Islands (JAPAN)

NORTH KOREA
Pyongyang
SOUTH KOREA
Seoul
Pusan

Dalian
Fushun
Harbin
Beijing
Qingdao
Yellow Sea
Nanjing
Shanghai

East China Sea

TAIWAN
Taipei

Tropic of Cancer

Hong Kong
Macao
Guangzhou
Hainan (CHINA)

PHILIPPINES
Manila

Celebes Sea

INDONESIA

Ujung Pandang
Surabaya
Jakarta
Bandung
Java Sea

Medan
MALAYSIA
SINGAPORE
Singapore
Kuala Lumpur
BRUNEI
Bandar Seri Begawan

Yakutsk

Harbin

Fushun

Wuhan
Chongqing
Chengdu
CHINA

Ulaanbaatar
MONGOLIA

Irkutsk

Lake Baykal

Novosibirsk

RUSSIA

Moscow

URAL MOUNTAINS

Yekaterinburg
Chelyabinsk
Omsk
Astana
KAZAKHSTAN
Aral Sea
Lake Balkhash
Almaty
Bishkek
KYRGYZSTAN
Tashkent
UZBEKISTAN
TAJIKISTAN
Dushanbe
TURKMENISTAN
Ashgabat
Kabul
AFGHANISTAN
Islamabad
Lahore
Delhi
New Delhi
PAKISTAN
Karachi
Jaipur
Ahmadabad
Mumbai (Bombay)
INDIA
Bangalore
Lakshadweep Islands (INDIA)
Chennai (Madras)
Bangalore

NEPAL
Kathmandu
BHUTAN
Thimphu
BANGLADESH
Dhaka
Kolkata (Calcutta)
Mandalay
MYANMAR (BURMA)
Yangon (Rangoon)
Bay of Bengal
Andaman Islands (INDIA)
Nicobar Islands (INDIA)
SRI LANKA
Colombo
MALDIVES
Male
Andaman Sea

LAOS
Vientiane
THAILAND
Bangkok
CAMBODIA
Phnom Penh
VIETNAM
Hanoi
Ho Chi Minh City
Gulf of Thailand
South China Sea

INDIAN OCEAN

Caspian Sea
Baku
AZERBAIJAN
Tehran
IRAN
Shiraz
GEORGIA
Tbilisi
ARMENIA
Yerevan
Mosul
Baghdad
IRAQ
Basra
KUWAIT
Kuwait City
Manama
BAHRAIN
QATAR
Doha
Riyadh
SAUDI ARABIA
Mecca
Jidda
Abu Dhabi
UNITED ARAB EMIRATES
Masqat (Muscat)
OMAN
Socotra (YEMEN)
Persian Gulf

Black Sea
Istanbul
Ankara
TURKEY
Izmir
CYPRUS
Nicosia
LEBANON
Beirut
SYRIA
Damascus
ISRAEL
Tel Aviv
Jerusalem
Amman
JORDAN

YEMEN
Sanaa
Gulf of Aden
Red Sea

AFRICA

Mediterranean Sea

Arabian Sea

Arctic Circle

North Pole

Barents Sea
Kara Sea

Africa: Physical

EUROPE

SOUTHWEST ASIA

Azores

Madeira Islands

Strait of Gibraltar

Mediterranean Sea

Gulf of Sidra

QATTARA DEPRESSION

Suez Canal

Persian Gulf

Canary Islands

ATLAS MOUNTAINS

Tropic of Cancer

Cape Blanc

EL DJOUF

S A H A R A

AHAGGAR MOUNTAINS

AIR MTS.

TIBESTI MOUNTAINS

LIBYAN DESERT

Nile River

Lake Nasser

NUBIAN DESERT

Red Sea

Cape Verde Islands

Cape Verde

Senegal R.

Niger River

S A H E L

S U D A N

CHAD BASIN

Lake Chad

White Nile

Blue Nile

Lake Tana

Gulf of Aden

FOUTA DJALLON

White Volta R.

Black Volta R.

Lake Volta

Benue River

SUDAN BASIN

ETHIOPIAN HIGHLANDS

HORN OF AFRICA

SOMALI PENINSULA

Cape Palmas

Gulf of Guinea

ADAMAWA MTS.

Ubangi River

Congo River

Lake Albert

Lake Edward

EASTERN RIFT VALLEY

Lake Turkana

Mount Kenya 17,058 ft (5,199 m)

Cape Lopez

CONGO BASIN

Kasai River

Lake Kivu

Lake Victoria

SERENGETI PLAIN

MASAI STEPPE

Mount Kilimanjaro 19,340 ft (5,895 m)

INDIAN OCEAN

0° Equator

MITUMBA MOUNTAINS

WESTERN RIFT VALLEY

Lake Tanganyika

Zanzibar

Seychelles

Ascension

Cuanza River

Lake Rukwa

Lake Malawi (Nyasa)

Lake Mweru

Cape Delgado

Comoro Islands

ATLANTIC OCEAN

Lake Kariba

Zambezi River

Madagascar

Okavango Delta

Victoria Falls

Mozambique Channel

Mauritius

Réunion

NAMIB DESERT

KALAHARI BASIN

KALAHARI DESERT

Limpopo River

Orange River

Vaal River

GREAT KARROO

DRAKENSBERG MOUNTAINS

Cape of Good Hope

Tropic of Capricorn

ELEVATION

Feet	Meters
13,120	4,000
6,560	2,000
1,640	500
656	200
(Sea level) 0	0 (Sea level)
Below sea level	Below sea level

0   250   500 Miles

0   250   500 Kilometers

Projection: Azimuthal Equal-Area

Africa: Political

EUROPE

SOUTHWEST ASIA

Azores (PORTUGAL)

Madeira (PORTUGAL)

Strait of Gibraltar

Casablanca • Rabat

Algiers ✪ Tunis ✪

TUNISIA

Tripoli ✪

Mediterranean Sea

Canary Islands (SPAIN)

El Aaiún •

WESTERN SAHARA (Claimed by Morocco)

Tropic of Cancer

MOROCCO

ALGERIA

LIBYA

EGYPT

Alexandria •

Giza • ✪ Cairo

Red Sea

CAPE VERDE

Praia ✪

MAURITANIA

Nouakchott ✪

MALI

NIGER

CHAD

SUDAN

Khartoum ✪

ERITREA

Asmara ✪

Gulf of Aden

SENEGAL

Dakar ✪

GAMBIA

Banjul ✪

Bamako ✪

Niamey ✪

Lake Chad

N'Djamena ✪

DJIBOUTI

Djibouti ✪

GUINEA BISSAU

Bissau ✪

GUINEA

Conakry ✪

Freetown ✪

SIERRA LEONE

Monrovia ✪

LIBERIA

BURKINA FASO

Ouagadougou ✪

CÔTE D'IVOIRE

Yamoussoukro ✪

BENIN

TOGO

GHANA

Lomé ✪

Abidjan •

Accra ✪

NIGERIA

Abuja ✪

Lagos •

Porto-Novo ✪

ETHIOPIA

Addis Ababa ✪

SOMALIA

CENTRAL AFRICAN REPUBLIC

Bangui ✪

SOUTH SUDAN

Juba ✪

Mogadishu •

Gulf of Guinea

Malabo ✪

EQUATORIAL GUINEA

Yaoundé ✪

CAMEROON

UGANDA

Kampala ✪

KENYA

Nairobi ✪

SÃO TOMÉ AND PRÍNCIPE

São Tomé ✪

Equator

Libreville ✪

GABON

REPUBLIC OF THE CONGO

Kisangani •

RWANDA

Kigali ✪

Lake Victoria

Mombasa •

Pemba

Zanzibar

INDIAN OCEAN

Victoria ✪

SEYCHELLES

Brazzaville ✪

CABINDA (ANGOLA)

Kinshasa ✪

DEMOCRATIC REPUBLIC OF THE CONGO

Bujumbura ✪

BURUNDI

TANZANIA

Dodoma ✪

Lake Tanganyika

Dar es Salaam •

ATLANTIC OCEAN

Luanda ✪

Lubumbashi •

Lake Malawi (Nyasa)

COMOROS

Moroni ✪

St. Helena (U.K.)

ANGOLA

ZAMBIA

Lusaka ✪

MALAWI

Lilongwe ✪

Harare ✪

ZIMBABWE

MOZAMBIQUE

Antananarivo ✪

MAURITIUS

Port Louis ✪

NAMIBIA

Windhoek ✪

BOTSWANA

Gaborone ✪

Bulawayo •

MADAGASCAR

Réunion (FRANCE)

Tropic of Capricorn

Pretoria ✪

Maputo ✪

Johannesburg •

Mbabane ✪

SWAZILAND

Bloemfontein •

Maseru ✪

LESOTHO

SOUTH AFRICA

Cape Town ✪

Legend

✪ National capital

• Other city

0   250   500 Miles

0   250   500 Kilometers

Projection: Azimuthal Equal-Area

NORTH AMERICA

ASIA

The Pacific: Political

NORTH PACIFIC OCEAN

SOUTH PACIFIC OCEAN

Tropic of Cancer

0° Equator

Tropic of Capricorn

International Date Line

National capital
● **Other city**

1,000 Miles
500   1,000 Kilometers
500
0

Projection: Azimuthal Equal-Area

N
E
W
S

Hawaiian Islands

Hawaii (U.S.)

Midway Island (U.S.)

Johnston Island (U.S.)

Kingman Reef (U.S.)
Palmyra Island (U.S.)
Washington Fanning Island (U.S.)
Jarvis I. (U.S.)

Howland I. (U.S.)
Baker I. (U.S.)

McKean I.
Gardner
Phoenix Islands

KIRIBATI

Starbuck Island

Manihiki Island

Tokelau (N.Z.)

Cook Islands (NEW ZEALAND)

Marquesas Islands (FRANCE)

Tuamotu Archipelago (FRANCE)

French Polynesia

P O L Y N E S I A

Society Islands (FRANCE)
Tahiti (FRANCE)
Papeete

Tubuai Islands (FRANCE)

Rapa Island (FRANCE)

Easter Island (CHILE)

Pitcairn (U.K.)
Pitcairn Island
Ducie Island

Rarotonga Island

SAMOA
American Samoa
Pago Pago
Apia

Niue (N.Z.)

TONGA
Nuku'alofa

Kermadec Islands (N.Z.)

TUVALU
Funafuti

Wallis & Futuna (FR.)

FIJI
Suva

M E L A N E S I A

Norfolk Island (AUSTRALIA)

Auckland

Wellington
Christchurch

Chatham Islands (N.Z.)

North Island

South Island

NEW ZEALAND

Bounty Islands (N.Z.)

Auckland Islands (NEW ZEALAND)

Wake Island (U.S.)

MARSHALL ISLANDS
Eniwetok I.
Kwajalein Island
Majuro

Tarawa
Gilbert Islands

NAURU
Palikir

MICRONESIA

Truk Is.

Bonin Islands (JAPAN)

Volcano Islands (JAPAN)

Northern Marianas (U.S.)

Guam (U.S.)
Agana

FEDERATED STATES OF MICRONESIA

SOLOMON ISLANDS
Honiara
Guadalcanal I.

Bismarck Archipelago

PAPUA NEW GUINEA
Port Moresby

New Guinea

PALAU
Koror

VANUATU
Port-Vila
Espíritu Santo I.
Malekula I.

New Caledonia (FRANCE)
Noumea
Loyalty Islands (FRANCE)

Coral Sea

Arafura Sea

Timor Sea

Philippine Sea

South China Sea

Christmas Island (AUSTRALIA)

A U S T R A L I A

Darwin

Perth

Adelaide

Melbourne

Sydney
Canberra
Brisbane

Hobart

Tasman Sea

INDIAN OCEAN

135°W
150°W
165°W
180°
165°E
150°E
135°E
120°E

45°S
30°S
15°S
120°W

30°N
15°N

30°N
15°N
0°
15°S
30°S
45°S

The North Pole

0   200   400 Miles
0   200   400 Kilometers

Projection:
Polar Azimuthal Equidistant

EUROPE

Kara
Sea

Barents
Sea

Norwegian
Sea

Laptev
Sea

Greenland
Sea

ASIA

ARCTIC
OCEAN

North
Pole

Arctic Circle

Greenland
(DENMARK)

ATLANTIC
OCEAN

POLAR ICE PACK

International Date Line

North
Magnetic
Pole

Baffin
Bay

Beaufort
Sea

Bering Sea

NORTH
AMERICA

150°E
120°E
90°E
60°E
30°E
30°W
60°W
50°N
60°N
70°N
80°N
150°W
120°W
180°

The South Pole

SOUTHERN   OCEAN

SOUTH
AMERICA

International Date Line

Antarctic Circle

Amundsen
Sea

Bellingshausen Sea

Antarctic
Peninsula

POLAR ICE PACK

Ross
Sea

Marie Byrd Land

Vinson Massif
16,067 ft
(4,897 m)

Ellsworth Land

POLAR ICE PACK

PACIFIC
OCEAN

Ross
Ice Shelf

Ronne
Ice Shelf

Weddell
Sea

Edith Ronne Land

Filchner
Ice Shelf

Mount Markham
over 14,275 ft
(over 4,351 m)

South
Pole

Coats
Land

Adelie
Land

South
Magnetic
Pole

ANTARCTICA

ICE CAP

ATLANTIC
OCEAN

WILKES LAND

QUEEN MAUD LAND

Shackleton
Ice Shelf

American
Highland

Enderby
Land

INDIAN OCEAN

SOUTHERN   OCEAN

0   250   500 Miles
0   250   500 Kilometers

Projection:
Polar Azimuthal Equidistant

150°W
120°W
90°W
60°W
30°W
0°
180°
150°E
120°E
60°S
70°S
80°S
50°S
30°E
60°E
90°E

Gazetteer

GAZETTEER

A

Afghanistan a landlocked country in Central Asia (p. 125)

Africa the second-largest continent; surrounded by the Atlantic Ocean, Indian Ocean, and Mediterranean Sea (p. 126)

Amazon River a major river in South America (p. 120)

Andes a mountain range along the west coast of South America (p. 120)

Antarctica the continent around the South Pole (p. 129)

Antarctic Circle the line of latitude located at 66.5° south of the equator; parallel beyond which no sunlight shines on the June solstice (p. 129)

Arctic Circle the line of latitude located at 66.5° north of the equator; parallel beyond which no sunlight shines on the December solstice (p. 129)

Arctic Ocean the ocean north of the Arctic Circle; the world's fourth-largest ocean (p. 114)

Asia the world's largest continent; located between Europe and the Pacific Ocean (p. 124)

Atlantic Ocean the ocean between the continents of North and South America and the continents of Europe and Africa; the world's second-largest ocean (p. 114)

Australia the only country occupying an entire continent (also called Australia); located between the Indian Ocean and the Pacific Ocean (p. 128)

C

California a state on the west coast of the United States (p. 112)

Canada the country north of the United States that occupies most of northern North America (p. 119)

Caribbean Sea an arm of the Atlantic Ocean between North and South America (p. 118)

Chicago (42°N, 88°W) a major city on Lake Michigan in northern Illinois (p. 113)

China a country in East Asia; the most populous country in the world (p. 125)

Colorado a state in the western United States (p. 112)

Cuba a Communist country and the largest island in the Caribbean Sea (p. 119)

E, F

Eastern Hemisphere the half of the globe between the prime meridian and 180° longitude that includes most of Africa and Europe as well as Asia, Australia, and the Indian Ocean (p. H7)

Egypt a country in North Africa between Libya and the Red Sea (p. 127)

equator the imaginary line of latitude that circles the globe halfway between the North and South Poles (p. H6)

Euphrates River a river in Southwest Asia (p. 124)

Europe the continent between the Ural Mountains and the Atlantic Ocean (p. 122)

Florida a state in the southern United States bordered mostly by the Atlantic Ocean and Gulf of Mexico (p. 113)

G, H, I

Grand Canyon a large canyon in the southwestern United States (p. 110)

Great Lakes the largest freshwater lake system in the world; located in North America (p. 111)

Great Plains a grassland region in the central United States (p. 111)

Gulf Stream a warm ocean current that flows north along the east coast of the United States (p. 52)

Hawaii an island state of the United States located in the Pacific Ocean (p. 112)

Himalayas a mountain system in Asia; the world's highest mountains (p. 124)

India a country in South Asia (p. 125)

Indian Ocean the world's third-largest ocean; located east of Africa, south of Asia, and west of Australia (p. 115)

Iraq a country located between Iran and Saudi Arabia in Southwest Asia (p. 125)

Italy a country in Southern Europe (p. 123)

J, K, L

Japan an island country in East Asia (p. 125)

Kenya a country in East Africa, south of Ethiopia (p. 127)

London (52°N, 0°) the capital of the United Kingdom (p. 123)

Mariana Trench the world's deepest ocean trench; located in the Pacific Ocean (p. 37)

Mediterranean Sea a sea surrounded by Europe, Asia, and Africa (p. 115)

Mexico a country in North America, south of the United States (p. 119)

Michigan a state in the north-central region of the United States (p. 113)

Mid-Atlantic Ridge a mid-ocean ridge located in the Atlantic Ocean (p. 37)

Mississippi River a major river in the central United States (p. 111)

Mount Saint Helens (46°N, 122°W) a volcano in Washington State; it erupted in 1980 (p. 43)

New York (41°N, 74°W) a city in the northeastern United States; the largest city in the United States (p. 113)

Nile River the world's longest river; flows through East Africa, Egypt, and into the Mediterranean Sea (p. 126)

North America a continent including Canada, the United States, Mexico, Central America, and the Caribbean islands (p. 119)

North Atlantic Current a warm ocean current that flows across the Atlantic Ocean and along Western Europe (p. 52)

Northern Hemisphere the northern half of the globe, between the equator and the North Pole (p. H7)

North Pole (90°N) the northern point of Earth's axis (p. 129)

Pacific Ocean the world's largest ocean; located between Asia and the Americas (p. 115)

prime meridian an imaginary line that runs through Greenwich, England, at 0° longitude (p. H6)

Ring of Fire a region that circles the Pacific Ocean; known for its earthquakes and volcanoes (p. 42)

Rocky Mountains a major mountain range in western North America (p. 110)

S

Sahara a desert in northern Africa; it is the largest desert in the world (p. 126)

San Andreas Fault an area at the boundary of the Pacific tectonic plate where earthquakes are common; located in California (p. 38)

Saudi Arabia a country occupying much of the Arabian Peninsula in Southwest Asia (p. 125)

Scandinavia a region of islands and peninsulas in far northern Europe; includes the countries of Norway, Sweden, Finland, and Denmark (p. 123)

South America a continent in the Western and Southern hemispheres (p. 121)

Southern Hemisphere the southern half of the globe, between the equator and the South Pole (p. H7)

South Pole (90°S) the southern point of Earth's axis (p. 129)

T

Texas a state in the southern United States (p. 113)

Tigris River a river in Southwest Asia (p. 124)

Tropic of Cancer the parallel 23.5° north of the equator; parallel on the globe at which the sun's most direct rays strike Earth during the June solstice (p. 28)

Tropic of Capricorn the parallel at 23.5° south of the equator; parallel on the globe at which the sun's most direct rays strike Earth during the December solstice (p. 28)

U, W

United States a country in North America located between Canada and Mexico (p. 112)

Washington a state in the northwestern United States (p. 112)

Washington, D.C. (39°N, 77°W) the capital of the United States (p. 113)

Western Hemisphere the half of the globe between 180° and the prime meridian that includes North and South America and the Pacific and Atlantic oceans (p. H7)

GAZETTEER

English and Spanish Glossary

MARK	AS IN	RESPELLING	EXAMPLE
a	<u>a</u>lphabet	a	*AL-fuh-bet
ā	<u>A</u>sia	ay	AY-zhuh
ä	c<u>a</u>rt, t<u>o</u>p	ah	KAHRT, TAHP
e	l<u>e</u>t, t<u>e</u>n	e	LET, TEN
ē	<u>e</u>ven, l<u>ea</u>f	ee	EE-vuhn, LEEF
i	<u>i</u>t, t<u>i</u>p, Br<u>i</u>t<u>i</u>sh	i	IT, TIP, BRIT-ish
ī	s<u>i</u>te, b<u>uy</u>, Oh<u>i</u>o	y	SYT, BY, oh-HY-oh
	<u>i</u>r<u>i</u>s	eye	EYE-ris
k	<u>c</u>ard	k	KAHRD
kw	<u>qu</u>est	kw	KWEST
ō	<u>o</u>ver, rainb<u>ow</u>	oh	OH-vuhr, RAYN-boh
ù	b<u>oo</u>k, w<u>oo</u>d	ooh	BOOHK, WOOHD
ò	<u>a</u>ll, <u>o</u>rchid	aw	AWL, AWR-kid
òi	f<u>oi</u>l, c<u>oi</u>n	oy	FOYL, KOYN
aù	<u>ou</u>t	ow	OWT
ə	c<u>u</u>p, b<u>u</u>tt<u>e</u>r	uh	KUHP, BUHT-uhr
ü	r<u>u</u>le, f<u>oo</u>d	oo	ROOL, FOOD
yü	f<u>ew</u>	yoo	FYOO
zh	vi<u>s</u>ion	zh	VIZH-uhn

*A syllable printed in small capital letters receives heavier emphasis than the other syllable(s) in a word.

Phonetic Respelling and Pronunciation Guide

Many of the key terms in this textbook have been respelled to help you pronounce them. The letter combinations used in the respelling throughout the narrative are explained in this phonetic respelling and pronunciation guide. The guide is adapted from Merriam-Webster's Collegiate Dictionary, Eleventh Edition; Merriam-Webster's Geographical Dictionary; and Merriam-Webster's Biographical Dictionary.

A

absolute location a specific description of where a place is located; absolute location is often expressed using latitude and longitude (p. 12)

ubicación absoluta descripción específica del lugar donde se ubica un punto; con frecuencia se define en términos de latitud y longitud (pág. 12)

B

birthrate the annual number of births per 1,000 people (p. 88)

índice de natalidad número de nacimientos por cada 1,000 personas en un año (pág. 88)

C

cartography the science of making maps (p. 19)

cartografía ciencia de crear mapas (pág. 19)

climate a region's average weather conditions over a long period of time (p. 50)

clima condiciones del tiempo promedio de una región durante un período largo de tiempo (pág. 50)

command economy an economic system in which the central government makes all economic decisions (p. 94)

economía autoritaria sistema económico en el que el gobierno central toma todas las decisiones económicas (pág. 94)

communism a political system in which the government owns all property and dominates all aspects of life in a country (p. 92)
comunismo sistema político en el que el gobierno es dueño de toda la propiedad y controla todos los aspectos de la vida de un país (pág. 92)

continent a large landmass that is part of Earth's crust; geographers identify seven continents (p. 36)
continente gran masa de tierra que forma parte de la corteza terrestre; los geógrafos identifican siete continentes (pág. 36)

cultural diffusion the spread of culture traits from one region to another (p. 85)
difusión cultural difusión de rasgos culturales de una región a otra (pág. 85)

cultural diversity having a variety of cultures in the same area (p. 83)
diversidad cultural existencia de una variedad de culturas en la misma zona (pág. 83)

culture the set of beliefs, values, and practices that a group of people have in common (p. 80)
cultura conjunto de creencias, valores y costumbres compartidas por un grupo de personas (pág. 80)

culture region an area in which people have many shared culture traits (p. 82)
región cultural región en la que las personas comparten muchos rasgos culturales (pág. 82)

culture trait an activity or behavior in which people often take part (p. 81)
rasgo cultural actividad o conducta frecuente de las personas (pág. 81)

D

deforestation the clearing of trees (p. 69)
deforestación tala de árboles (pág. 69)

democracy a form of government in which the people elect leaders and rule by majority (p. 91)
democracia sistema de gobierno en el que el pueblo elige a sus líderes y gobierna por mayoría (pág. 91)

desertification the spread of desertlike conditions (p. 65)
desertificación ampliación de condiciones desérticas (pág. 65)

developed countries countries with strong economies and a high quality of life (p. 95)
países desarrollados países con economías sólidas y una alta calidad de vida (pág. 95)

developing countries countries with less productive economies and a lower quality of life (p. 95)
países en vías de desarrollo países con economías menos productivas y una menor calidad de vida (pág. 95)

E

earthquake a sudden, violent movement of Earth's crust (p. 38)
terremoto movimiento repentino y violento de la corteza terrestre (pág. 38)

ecosystem a group of plants and animals that depend on each other for survival, and the environment in which they live (p. 63)
ecosistema grupo de plantas y animales que dependen unos de otros para sobrevivir, y el ambiente en el que estos viven (pág. 63)

environment the land, water, climate, plants, and animals of an area; surroundings (pp. 12, 62)
ambiente la tierra, el agua, el clima, las plantas y los animales de una zona; los alrededores (págs. 12, 62)

erosion the movement of sediment from one location to another (p. 39)
erosión movimiento de sedimentos de un lugar a otro (pág. 39)

ENGLISH AND SPANISH GLOSSARY

ethnic group a group of people who share a common culture and ancestry (p. 83)
   grupo étnico grupo de personas que comparten una cultura y una ascendencia (pág. 83)

extinct no longer here; a species that has died out has become extinct (p. 64)
   extinto que ya no existe; una especie que ha desaparecido está extinta (pág. 64)

F

fossil fuels nonrenewable resources that formed from the remains of ancient plants and animals; coal, petroleum, and natural gas are all fossil fuels (p. 69)
   combustibles fósiles recursos no renovables formados a partir de restos de plantas y animales antiguos; el carbón, el petróleo y el gas natural son combustibles fósiles (pág. 69)

freshwater water that is not salty; it makes up only about 3 percent of our total water supply (p. 31)
   agua dulce agua que no es salada; representa sólo alrededor del 3 por ciento de nuestro suministro total de agua (pág. 31)

front the place where two air masses of different temperatures or moisture content meet (p. 53)
   frente lugar en el que se encuentran dos masas de aire con diferente temperatura o humedad (pág. 53)

G

geography the study of the world, its people, and the landscapes they create (p. 4)
   geografía estudio del mundo, de sus habitantes y de los paisajes creados por el ser humano (pág. 4)

glacier a large area of slow-moving ice (p. 31)
   glaciar gran bloque de hielo que avanza con lentitud (pág. 31)

globalization the process in which countries are increasingly linked to each other through culture and trade (p. 97)
   globalización proceso por el cual los países se encuentran cada vez más interconectados a través de la cultura y el comercio (pág. 97)

globe a spherical, or ball-shaped, model of the entire planet (p. 8)
   globo terráqueo modelo esférico, o en forma de bola, de todo el planeta (pág. 8)

groundwater water found below Earth's surface (p. 32)
   agua subterránea agua que se encuentra debajo de la superficie de la Tierra (pág. 32)

gross domestic product (GDP) the value of all goods and services produced within a country in a single year (p. 95)
   producto interior bruto (PIB) valor de todos los bienes y servicios producidos en un país durante un año (pág. 95)

H

habitat the place where a plant or animal lives (p. 64)
   hábitat lugar en el que vive una planta o animal (pág. 64)

human geography the study of the world's people, communities, and landscapes (p. 18)
   geografía humana estudio de los habitantes, las comunidades y los paisajes del mundo (pág. 18)

humanitarian aid assistance to people in distress (p. 100)
   ayuda humanitaria ayuda a personas en peligro (pág. 100)

humus (HYOO-muhs) decayed plant or animal matter; it helps soil support abundant plant life (p. 65)

humus materia animal o vegetal descompuesta; contribuye a que crezca una gran cantidad de plantas en el suelo (pág. 65)

hydroelectric power the production of electricity from waterpower, such as from running water (p. 70)

energía hidroeléctrica producción de electricidad generada por la energía del agua, como la del agua corriente (pág. 70)

I

interdependence a relationship between countries in which they rely on one another for resources, goods, or services (p. 99)

interdependencia una relación entre países en que dependen uno de otros para obtener recursos, bienes, o servicios (pág. 99)

L

landform a shape on the planet's surface, such as a mountain, valley, plain, island, or peninsula (p. 35)

accidente geográfico forma de la superficie terrestre, como una montaña, un valle, una llanura, una isla o una península (pág. 35)

landscape all the human and physical features that make a place unique (p. 4)

paisaje todas las características humanas y físicas que hacen que un lugar sea único (pág. 4)

latitude the distance north or south of Earth's equator (p. 27)

latitud distancia hacia el norte o el sur desde el ecuador (pág. 27)

lava magma that reaches Earth's surface (p. 37)

lava magma que llega a la superficie terrestre (pág. 37)

M

map a flat drawing that shows all or part of Earth's surface (p. 8)

mapa representación plana que muestra total o parcialmente la superficie de la Tierra (pág. 8)

market economy an economic system based on free trade and competition (p. 94)

economía de mercado sistema económico basado en el libre comercio y la competencia (pág. 94)

meteorology the study of weather and what causes it (p. 20)

meteorología estudio de las condiciones del tiempo y sus causas (pág. 20)

migration the movement of people from one place to live in another (p. 89)

migración movimiento de personas de un lugar para ir a vivir a otro lugar (pág. 89)

monsoon a seasonal wind that brings either dry or moist air (p. 58)

monzón viento estacional que trae aire seco o húmedo (pág. 58)

N

natural resource any material in nature that people use and value (p. 68)

recurso natural todo material de la naturaleza que las personas utilizan y valoran (pág. 68)

nonrenewable resource a resource that cannot be replaced naturally; coal and petroleum are examples of nonrenewable resources (p. 69)

recurso no renovable recurso que no puede reemplazarse naturalmente; el carbón y el petróleo son ejemplos de recursos no renovables (pág. 69)

O

ocean currents large streams of surface sea-water; they move heat around Earth (p. 52)
corrientes oceánicas grandes corrientes de agua de mar que fluyen en la superficie del océano; transportan calor por toda la Tierra (pág. 52)

P

permafrost permanently frozen layers of soil (p. 61)
permafrost capas de tierra congeladas permanentemente (pág. 61)

physical geography the study of the world's physical features—its landforms, bodies of water, climates, soils, and plants (p. 16)
geografía física estudio de las características físicas de la Tierra: sus accidentes geográficos, sus masas de agua, sus climas, sus suelos y sus plantas (pág. 16)

plate tectonics a theory suggesting that Earth's surface is divided into a dozen or so slow-moving plates, or pieces of Earth's crust (p. 36)
tectónica de placas teoría que sugiere que la superficie terrestre está dividida en unas doce placas, o fragmentos de corteza terrestre, que se mueven lentamente (pág. 36)

popular culture culture traits that are well known and widely accepted (p. 98)
cultura popular rasgos culturales conocidos y de gran aceptación (pág. 98)

population the total number of people in a given area (p. 86)
población número total de personas en una zona determinada (pág. 86)

population density a measure of the number of people living in an area (p. 86)
densidad de población medida del número de personas que viven en una zona (pág. 86)

precipitation water that falls to Earth's surface as rain, snow, sleet, or hail (p. 31)
precipitación agua que cae a la superficie de la Tierra en forma de lluvia, nieve, aguanieve o granizo (pág. 31)

prevailing winds winds that blow in the same direction over large areas of Earth (p. 51)
vientos preponderantes vientos que soplan en la misma dirección sobre grandes zonas de la Tierra (pág. 51)

R

reforestation planting trees to replace lost forestland (p. 69)
reforestación siembra de árboles para reemplazar los bosques que han desaparecido (pág. 69)

region a part of the world that has one or more common features that distinguish it from surrounding areas (p. 6)
región parte del mundo que tiene una o más características comunes que la distinguen de las áreas que la rodean (pág. 6)

relative location a general description of where a place is located; a place's relative location is often expressed in relation to something else (p. 12)
ubicación relativa descripción general de la posición de un lugar; la ubicación relativa de un lugar suele expresarse en relación con otra cosa (pág. 12)

renewable resource a resource that Earth replaces naturally, such as water, soil, trees, plants, and animals (p. 69)
recurso renovable recurso que la Tierra reemplaza por procesos naturales, como el agua, el suelo, los árboles, las plantas y los animales (pág. 69)

revolution the 365¼-day trip Earth takes around the sun each year (p. 27)
revolución viaje de 365¼ días que la Tierra hace alrededor del Sol cada año (pág. 27)

rotation one complete spin of Earth on its axis; each rotation takes about 24 hours (p. 26)
rotación giro completo de la Tierra sobre su propio eje; cada rotación toma 24 horas (pág. 26)

savanna an area of tall grasses and scattered trees and shrubs (p. 58)
sabana zona de pastos altos con arbustos y árboles dispersos (pág. 58)

social science a field that focuses on people and the relationships among them (p. 5)
ciencias sociales campo de estudio que se enfoca en las personas y en las relaciones entre ellas (pág. 5)

solar energy energy from the sun (p. 26)
energía solar energía del Sol (pág. 26)

steppe a semidry grassland or prairie; steppes often border deserts (p. 59)
estepa pradera semiárida; las estepas suelen encontrarse en el límite de los desiertos (pág. 59)

surface water water that is found in Earth's streams, rivers, and lakes (p. 31)
agua superficial agua que se encuentra en los arroyos, ríos y lagos de la Tierra (pág. 31)

T

tropics regions close to the equator (p. 29)
trópicos regiones cercanas al ecuador (pág. 29)

U

United Nations an organization of countries that promotes peace and security around the world (p. 99)
Naciones Unidas organización de países que promueve la paz y la seguridad en todo el mundo (pág. 99)

W

water cycle the movement of water from Earth's surface to the atmosphere and back (p. 33)
ciclo del agua circulación del agua desde la superficie de la Tierra hacia la atmósfera y de regreso a la Tierra (pág. 33)

water vapor water occurring in the air as an invisible gas (p. 32)
vapor de agua agua que se encuentra en el aire en estado gaseoso e invisible (pág. 32)

weather the short-term changes in the air for a given place and time (p. 50)
tiempo cambios a corto plazo en la atmósfera en un momento y lugar determinados (pág. 50)

weathering the process by which rock is broken down into smaller pieces (p. 39)
meteorización proceso de desintegración de las rocas en pedazos pequeños (pág. 39)

ENGLISH AND SPANISH GLOSSARY

Index

INDEX

mountains and, 54; water cycle and, 32–33f, 33
predators: in ecosystem, 63f
prevailing winds, 51–52, 51m
primary industry, 93, 93p
Primary Sources: *Charter of the United Nations, The,* 100; *Geography for Life,* 14; *Time Enough for Love,* 50
prime meridian, H2
projections. *See* map projections

quaternary industry, 93p, 94
Quick Facts: Climate, Environment, and Resources visual summary, 75; A Geographer's World visual summary, 21; Planet Earth visual summary, 45; The World's People visual summary, 101

rainfall: limits on life and, 62; seasons and, 29; tropics, 29
rain forests, 58; clearing, 64
rain shadow, 54, 54p
rate of natural increase, 88; Bangladesh, 90; Canada, 89–90; France, 90; Japan, 88; Mali, 88–89; Nigeria, 90
Reading Skills: Reading Social Studies, H14–H17; Understanding Cause and Effect, 48, 108; Understanding Main Ideas, 78, 109; Using Prior Knowledge, 2, 106; Using Word Parts, 24, 107
recreation: water and, 34
Red Cross, 100
reforestation, 69
region, 6–7
region theme, 10–12, 11f
relative location, 12
religion: development of culture and, 81
renewable energy resources, 70–71

renewable resources, 69
revolution of Earth, 27
Ring of Fire, 38, 42–43f
Rio de Janeiro, 41p
River, The **(Gary Paulsen),** 73
rivers, 31; defined, H10; erosion, 40, 40p
rock: in soil, 65p
rock formation: Arizona, 3p
Rocky Mountains, 6
Roman Catholic religion, 81
rotation of Earth, 26–27; prevailing winds, 52
runoff, 32–33f, 33
Russia: birthrate, 88; death rate, 88
Rwanda: ethnic group conflict, 83

Sahara, 6; culture and, 82; Tuareg, 58
salt water, 31, 31p
San Andreas Fault, 38
sand: wind erosion, 39, 39p
satellite images: analyzing, 15; as geographer's tool, 9; infrared images, 15, 15p; true color, 15, 15p
Saudi Arabia: government of, 92
savannas, 58
scale, map, H7
Scavenger Hunt, H22
science and technology: computer mapping, 19, 19m; soil factory, 64
seasons, 28–29; based on temperature and length of day, 28; midnight sun, 29, 29p; in Northern Hemisphere, 28; rainfall and, 29; solar energy and, 28–29; Southern Hemisphere, 28–29; spring and fall, 29; tilt of Earth and, 28–29; winter and summer, 28–29
secondary industry, 93, 93p
sediment, 40
Singapore, 103c
sinkhole: defined, H10
soccer: as cultural trait, 81
social science, 5

Social Studies Skills
Chart and Graph Skills: Analyzing a Bar Graph, 74
Geography Skills: Analyzing Satellite Images, 15; Using a Physical Map, 44
Study Skills: Organizing Information, 96
Social Studies Words, H18
soil: environments, 64–65; humus, 64, 65; layers of, 65p; limits on life and, 62; losing fertility, 65; as renewable resource, 69; soil factory, 64
solar energy, 45p; defined, 27; in ecosystem, 63, 63f; movement of Earth and, 27; as renewable energy, 71; seasons and, 28–29; water cycle and, 32–33f, 33; weather and climate, 51
South America: Andes, 37; climate zones of, 56m; energy production, 70c; South America: Physical, 120m; South America: Political, 121m
South American plate, 36p, 37
Southeast Asia: language and landforms, 40; terrace farming, 40–41
Southern Hemisphere: defined, H3; map of, H3; seasons in, 28–29
South Pole: climate, 61; prevailing winds, 52; The Sorth Pole, 129m
Southwest Asia: Arab culture region, 82, 82m, 82p
Southwestern United States, 33
Spain: government of, 92
special-purpose maps, H9
spring, 29
springs: groundwater and, 32
Standardized Test Practice, 23, 47, 77, 103
steppe climate, 59; average annual precipitation, 74c; overview of, 56c
storm surges, 54
strait: defined, H10
stratovolcanoes, 43
streams, 31
Study Skills: Organizing Information, 96

Credits and Acknowledgments

HISTORY Unless otherwise indicated below, all video reference screens are © 2010 A&E Television Networks, LLC. All rights reserved.

For permission to reproduce copyrighted material, grateful acknowledgment is made to the following sources:

National Geographic Society: From *Geography for Life: National Geography Standards 1994.* Copyright © 1994 by National Geographic Research & Exploration. All rights reserved.

G. P. Putnam's Sons, a division of Penguin Group (USA) Inc.: From *Time Enough for Love, the Lives of Lazarus Long* by Robert Heinlein. Copyright © 1973 by Robert Heinlein. All rights reserved.

Random House Children's Books, a division of Random House, Inc.: From *The River* by Gary Paulsen. Copyright © 1991 by Gary Paulsen.

United Nations: From the *Preamble to the Charter of the United Nations.* Copyright © 1945 by United Nations.

Sources used by The World Almanac® for charts and graphs:

Eruptions in the Ring of Fire: *The World Almanac and Book of Facts, 2005*; World Energy Production: Energy Information Administration of the U.S. Department of Energy; A Developed and a Developing Country: *The World Factbook, 2005*; U.S. Census Bureau; World Health Organization

Illustrations and Photo Credits

Cover: (l), David C. Ellis/Getty Images; (r), Nick Tapp/Lonely Planet Images.

Front Matter: ii, Victoria Smith/HMH; iv, Sharna Balfour/Gallo Images/Corbis; vi, Liu Liqun/Corbis vii, Eric Meola/Getty Images; viii, Planetary Visions; ix, Tom Nebia/Corbis; H16 (t), Earth Satellite Corporation/Photo Researchers, Inc.; H16 (tc), Frans Lemmens/Getty Images; H16 (c), London Aerial Photo Library/Corbis; H16 (bc), Harvey Schwartz/Index Stock Imagery/Fotosearch; H16 (b), Tom Nebbia/Corbis.

Introduction: A, Taxi/Getty Images; B (bkgd), Planetary Visions; B (cr), Frans Lemmens/Image Bank/Getty Images; B (bl), Michael Melford/Getty Images; 1 (bc), Robert Harding/Digital Vision/Getty Images.

Chapter 1: 2 (br), M. Colonel/Photo Researchers, Inc.; 2-3 (t), Age Fotostock/SuperStock; 3 (br), Anthony Cassidy/Getty Images; 3 (bl), Digital Vision/Getty Images; 5 (b), Frans Lemmens/Getty Images; 6 (b), Kim Sayer/Corbis; 7 (br), ESA/K.Horgan/Getty Images; 7 (bl), London Aerial Photo Library/Corbis; 8 (tl), Michael Newman/PhotoEdit; 11 (br), Morton Beebe/Corbis; 11 (bc), AFP/Getty Images; 11 (tr), Miles Ertman/Masterfile; 11 (tl), David R. Frazier/Photo Researchers, Inc.; 11 (bl), Corbis; 12-13 (br), Tom Nebbia/Corbis; 15 (l), M-SAT Ltd./Science Photo Library; 15 (r), Earth Satellite Corporation/Science Photo Library; 17 (tr), Penny Tweedie/Stone/Getty Images; 17 (tl), Torleif Svensson/Corbis; 19 (b), Donna Cox and Robert Patterson/NCSA; 20 (tl), Joe Raedle/Getty Images; 21 (tr), Donna Cox and Robert Patterson/NCSA; 21 (tc), Penny Tweedie/Stone/Getty Images; 21 (tl), Frans Lemmens/Getty Images.

Chapter 2: 24 (br), Pete Saloutos/Corbis; 24-25 (t), Earth Satellite Corporation/Science Photo Library; 25 (tr), 2010 A&E Television Networks, LLC. All rights reserved; 25 (bl), George H.H. Huey/Corbis; 25 (br), Royalty-Free/Corbis; 29 (tr), Paul A. Souders/Corbis; 30-31 (b), Doug Wilson/Corbis; 31 (br), Terje Rakke/The Image Bank/Getty Images; 34 (tr), Alan Sirulnikoff/Photo Researchers, Inc.; 34 (tl), Rick Doyle/Corbis; 37 (bl), Bettmann/Corbis; 38 (cr), Yann Arthus-Bertrand/Corbis; 38 (br), Roger Cracknell 01/classic/Alamy; 39 (br), Age Fotostock/SuperStock; 40 (bl), Owaki-Kulla/Corbis; 41 (t), Age Fotostock/SuperStock; 43 (tr), Gary Braasch/Corbis; 43 (tl), David Weintraub/Photo Researchers, Inc.; 45 (tr), Galen Rowell/Corbis; 45 (tc), Rick Doyle/Corbis; 45 (tl), W.H. Mueller/Zefa Images/Corbis; 45 (tr), Roger Cracknell 01/classic/Alamy.

Chapter 3: 48 (br), Kate Thompson/National Geographic/Getty Images; 48-49 (t), Warren Faidley/WeatherStock; 49 (tr), 2010 A&E Television Networks, LLC. All rights reserved; 49 (br), Bill Ross/Corbis; 49 (bl), L. Clarke/Corbis; 53 (br), Eric Meola/Getty Images; 53 (tr), William Thomas Cain/Getty Images; 56 (tl), Age FotoStock/SuperStock; 57 (cr), Royalty-free/Corbis; 57 (tr), Corbis; 58 (cl), Martin Harvey/Corbis; 59 Ingram/PictureQuest/Jupiterimages; 60 (t), Sharna Balfour/Gallo Images/Corbis; 64 (b), Carl and Ann Purcell/Corbis; 69 (c), Adrian Arbib/Corbis; 69 (tr), William Campbell/Peter Arnold, Inc.; 71 (tr), James L. Amos/Corbis; 71 (cr), Charles Bowman/Photolibrary; 72 (tl), Sarah Leen/National Geographic Image Collection; 73 (tr), James Randklev/Getty Images; 75 (tr), James L. Amos/Corbis; 75 (tl), Royalty-free/Corbis.

Chapter 4: 78 (b), Liu Liqun/Corbis; 78-79 (t), Getty Images; 79 (br), Shahn Rowe/Stone/Getty Images; 79 (bl), Richard I'Anson/Lonely Planet Images; 81 (tr), Knut Mueller/Das Fotoarchiv/Photolibrary; 81 (tl), Tom Wagner/Corbis; 83 (bl), Peter Armenia; 83 (r), Photononstop/SuperStock; 84 (cr), Timothy A. Clary/AFP/Getty Images; 84 (cl), Reuters/Corbis; 84-85 (t), Courtesy Library of Congress; 89 (t), The Granger Collection; 90 (tr), Peter Beck/Corbis; 90 (cr), Karen Kasmauski/Corbis; 93 (b), Michelle Garrett/Corbis; 93 (bc), Kevin Fleming/Corbis; 93 (t), Owaki-Kulla/Corbis; 93 (tc), Jack Sullivan/Alamy; 94 (br), Carl & Ann Purcell/Corbis; 94 (bl), Glen Allison/Stone/Getty Images; 101 (tr), Reuters/Corbis; 101 (tl), Sebastian Bolesch/Peter Arnold, Inc.; 101 (tl), Photononstop/SuperStock; 101 (tc), Jack Sullivan/Alamy.

Staff Credits

The people who contributed to *Holt McDougal: Introduction to Geography* are listed below. They represent editorial, design, production, emedia, and permissions.

Melanie Baccus, Angela Beckmann, Julie Beckman-Key, Genick Blaise, Ed Blake, Jennifer Campbell, Henry Clark, Grant Davidson, Nina Degollado, Rose Degollado, Christine Devall, Michelle Dike, Lydia Doty, Chase Edmond, Susan Franques, Stephanie Friedman,Bob Fullilove, Matthew Gierhart, Bill Gillis, Ann Gorbett, Janet Harrington, Betsy Harris, Wendy Hodge, Tim Hovde, Cathy Jenevein, Carrie Jones, Kadonna Knape, David Knowles, Aylin Koker, Laura Lasley, Sarah Lee, Sean McCormick, Joe Melomo, Richard Metzger, Andrew Miles, Joeleen Ornt, Debra O'Shields, Jarred Prejean, Paul Provence, Shelly Ramos, Curtis Riker, Michelle Rimsa, Michael Rinella, Jennifer Rockwood, Carole Rollins, Beth Sample, Annette Saunders, Jenny Schaeffer, Kay Selke, Chris Smith, Jeremy Strykul, Jeannie Taylor, Terri Taylor, Joni Wackwitz, Mary Wages, Diana Holman Walker, Nadyne Wood, Robin Zaback